THE
DENBY DALE
PIES

'Ten Giants' 1788–2000

THE
DENBY DALE
PIES

'Ten Giants' 1788–2000

CHRIS HEA H

Wharncliffe Books

First published in Great Britain in 2012 by
Wharncliffe Books
an imprint of
Pen & Sword Books Ltd
47 Church Street
Barnsley
South Yorkshire
S70 2AS

ISBN 978 1 84563 153 6

A CIP catalogue record for this book is
available from the British Library

Typeset in 9.5/12pt Palatino by Chic Media Ltd

Printed and bound in England
by CPI Group (UK) Ltd, Croydon, CR0 4YY

Pen & Sword Books Ltd incorporates the imprints of
Pen & Sword Aviation, Pen & Sword Family History, Pen & Sword Maritime,
Pen & Sword Military, Pen & Sword Discovery, Wharncliffe Local History,
Wharncliffe True Crime, Wharncliffe Transport, Pen & Sword Select,
Pen & Sword Military Classics, Leo Cooper, Remember When,
The Praetorian Press, Seaforth Publishing and Frontline Publishing

For a complete list of Pen & Sword titles please contact
PEN & SWORD BOOKS LIMITED
47 Church Street, Barnsley, South Yorkshire, S70 2AS, England
E-mail: enquiries@pen-and-sword.co.uk
Website: www.pen-and-sword.co.uk

Contents

Dedication

For Seren

diligo, vires quod sodalitas

Acknowledgements

My thanks go to:

John Colledge at Denby Dale Pie Hall, Amanda Booth and Katina Bill at the Tolson Museum, Kirklees Libraries & Local Studies (website), Gordon Robinson (sadly, now deceased), Mabeth Robinson, Bella Falk of Love Productions Television, Charles Hewitt, Jonathan Wright, Bryan Heath, Paul Heath, Richard Nicholls (for inspiring and producing an earlier incarnation of this work), Stephen Carter (*Huddersfield Examiner*), Jonathan Wilkinson, Roni Wilkinson, Mary Fisher, John Hirst, Richard Netherwood, James Hinchliffe, Malcolm Eastwood, Peter Buckley, Brian Buckley, Neil Tann, Sheila Netherwood, Andrew Pinfield, Dean, Tony and Celia Wyatt and Lucy Sylvia Menzies-Earl.

Special thanks to my mum, Carol Heath, without whose help and enthusiasm this book would have had far fewer photographs. Madge Greaves, for not only taking the trouble to keep two large scrapbooks as a memento of her role in the 1964 Pie, but allowing me to make full use of them. Finally, Susan Buckley, whose passion for local history and the pies had led to her amassing a large collection of memorabilia. Her trust and co-operation were very gratefully received.

I cannot tell you the wherefore or why,
They honour events by making a pie,
Except it be the fresh breeze from the hills,
That works on their stomachs like camomile pills,
So making them just as hungry as owt-
And hunger at times is productive of thowt.

Any opinions, errors or omissions are entirely those of the author. Whilst every effort has been made to trace the copyright owners of the illustrations in this book the author wishes to apologise to anyone who has not been acknowledged.

It has been extremely difficult in some cases to determine the origin of copyright on photographs and newspaper cuttings. All original photographs have been checked for references on the reverse side but in most cases they were blank. The same applies to newspaper cuttings, which do not include the name of the paper. Where copyright is known this has been acknowledged. I would beg the indulgence of any affronted party if an error has occurred and will happily correct this in any subsequent reprint of this work.

Some of the photographs in this work have been reproduced courtesy of the Kirklees Image Archive Photographic Website. This is an excellent service and for those interested, copies of these particular photographs can be purchased from here: kirkleesimages.org.uk.

Words of Wisdom from Denby Dale

'That's t'field wheere t'big pawoi wor. Theere were three whawl sheep an' a
cawf e wun pawoi! What wur it for? Whawoi, rejoicin' at Corn Bill cummin off e '46.
T'pawoi weighed ten hunderd weight. They lawoik pawoi, men e Denby Daal'.

Taken from the *Barnsley Chronicle* dated 27 August 1887. The latter is a literal rendition of an item of local historical information communicated to the late Mr W S Banks, author of walks in Yorkshire, by a native on the occasion of a visit to Denby Dale during the summer of 1868.

•

'If you are Englishmen, stand back.'

John Brierley 1887.

•

An enthusiastic Denby Daler declares that the pie at present in hand will make some
poor poet – 'awther throw hissen into bed ovver it, or else he'll split a gusset!'

Leeds Mercury 1928.

•

'T pie's bigger then thou thawt'

Observed by a worthy Yorkshire visitor on seeing that the Pie was stuck in the oven.
Sheffield Daily Telegraph 1928.

•

'We have delivered the goods', declared the chairman, Mr W A Heap . . .
'Not before time awther!' was the bawled comment returned.

Huddersfield Examiner 1928.

•

'Ger into that pie!'

Shouted by a famished interrupter during the speeches in 1928.

•

'It's ready . . . and it's champion!'

Mr Jack Hirst, butcher, Denby Dale, 1964.

Introduction

The Village of Denby Dale has ancient links to the arts of pie making. The first of its giant pies was reputedly baked in 1788, though it is perfectly feasible that there were others prior to this. Whether earlier ones may have been baked to celebrate a national or international event or were simply the results of a good harvest safely gathered in will probably never be known. Today, the baking of monster pies in the village has a national reputation, a unique claim to fame, hence the boasts made by the signposts as one enters the village.

Nestling between the West Yorkshire towns of Huddersfield and Wakefield and the South Yorkshire town of Barnsley, Denby Dale is today a relatively quiet, semi-rural village, of just over 2,000 people.

The village was born of the industrial revolution. Originally known as Denby Dykeside or simply Dykeside, isolated farms and cottages separated the villages of Denby & Cumberworth, which were both mentioned in the Domesday Survey of 1086. The 'dyke' in Dykeside was the River Dearne, which provided power for corn mills and later factories, that caused the beginnings of the settlement we know today. The oldest of three corn mills dated back to before 1546.

The lords of the manor of Denby during the twelfth and thirteenth centuries were initially a family named after the area, the de Denbys. The lordship passed from them by marriage to the Burdet family, originally of Rande in Lincolnshire, in about 1305. The Burdet's became related, again by marriage, to the Balliol family, once Scottish Royalty. It was King Edward I who placed John Balliol on the throne of Scotland, only to remove him when he became less than compliant. The Burdet's were heavily involved in the politics and military action undertaken by the English King during the Scottish wars and a marriage between Robert Burdet and Idonea Balliol sealed the alliance. Indeed, for a time, Sir Robert Balliol, Idonea's father, held the lordship of Denby himself. The Burdet family retained the lordship until 1616 when it was sold to Sir William Savile of Thornhill. The Savile family then held the lordship until the twentieth century.

The village's isolation began to end with the coming of two turnpike roads (the A635 and A636), the textile industry and the railway. The railway facilitated and serviced the textile industry and the arrival of the mills of Z Hinchliffe & Sons in 1850, Jonas Kenyon & Sons in 1854, and John Brownhill & Sons in 1868 provided employment for a greatly expanding population. Gradually the occupants of the hill villages such as Denby drifted away from home -based spinning and weaving to work in these factories, bringing with them their ready knowledge of the industry. Here in the village were people with skill inherited from centuries of handling fleeces, yarns and cloths, however plain and rough the products might be. Wool was readily available to process, as was water for washing and dying, coal for heat and stone for building. From this time the hill villages lost their importance and the previously tiny hamlet known as Denby Dyke or Dykeside grew steadily, its population increasing and its name changing to Denby Dale some time around 1815.

Agriculture and textiles were the predominant occupations in the district, indeed many weavers had a smallholding and many farmers owned weaving looms and it was into this environment that the Denby Dale pies made their formal entry into history.

The early pie events, though somewhat unusual, were very much local, social celebrations. By the late Victorian era pie proceedings tended to be led largely by the local mill owners and religious and business leaders. Many members of the committees (though not all) were their employees, their positions on the committee relating to their equivalent positions in their employment, following the social structure of the time. This can be seen in the dress code reflected in the photographs that have survived. These pies were made during an age that was yet to experience the horrors of two world wars. Britain at the time was a world leader both militarily and in manufacturing, its empire stretched around the world leading many to prosperity and embracing the endeavour shown by the emerging middle classes. Amidst this success there was also poverty and suffering countrywide.

Some of the inhabitants of Denby Dykeside and its near neighbours at Upper Denby and Cumberworth experienced extreme poverty during the nineteenth century. As the mills became established cottage-based weaving went into serious decline and the foundation of the workhouse at Upper Denby in 1827 illustrates the difficulties faced by many large families with little or no way to provide for themselves or their numerous children. When the Denby workhouse closed in around 1849, the Penistone Union workhouse took over and continued to care for the poor until after the Second World War.

Celebrations based upon food of the gargantuan Denby Dale variety may have been seen by the more unfortunate as a slap across the face given by those living in circumstances far better than their own. To compensate for this we should remember that the pies were highly special and very irregular occasions and that the organisers did make provision for the poor and for children to enjoy their share of the day and, of course, of the pie. It is likely that, in the main, the poor and underprivileged looked forward to the day with as much enthusiasm as everyone else. It was an opportunity to enjoy themselves and to leave their troubles at home, even if only for a very short while.

The mill owners and manufacturers continued to be involved with the organisation of the pies up to and including the 1964 event, though it must be said that to organise an event on this scale, their connections and pulling power proved invaluable in initially getting the project off the ground. As always they were assisted by the farmers, landowners, cattle breeders and crop growers but the pies were becoming huge, and so were the financial implications for what was once a small village concern.

In 1964 there were dissenting voices issuing complaints to the effect that so much of the basis for the celebrations that year (including ingredients) were coming from outside the district. For local farmers to supply such a huge amount of beef (let alone other ingredients) was simply not practical any more. A more cynical view might be that, from this point on the pies have become more of a corporate event, the highest bidding sponsors achieving the maximum amount of publicity no matter where their origins or premises. The fact is that the pie is still a Denby Dale tradition, it has the ability to attract the funding of organisations that

Denby Dale, circa 1920. Brownhill's, Springfield Mill is in the background, along with the terraced houses on Sunny Bank. A row of cottages demolished during the 1970s can be seen in the foreground. *(Courtesy of Old Barnsley.)*

would otherwise have never heard of this tiny former mill village. It could be said that it is only because of this funding that the last three events were able to take place at all and it is a credit to each respective pie committee that they were successful in achieving their aims. So what if there are sponsors' names on the pie dish, the napkins, the sauce, the marquees and suchlike? If this is the way forward, and if it allows the village its once a generation or so claim to international fame, then it is a small price to pay.

As the twenty-first century sees more and more globalisation, individuality is becoming less apparent. The need for increased housing to accommodate a rapidly growing population is seeing many small villages being swallowed up by new estates and, in many cases, their individual characteristics and personalities are lost along the way. Perhaps the baking of giant pies in Denby Dale is an odd, quirky tradition, but it is to be hoped that it is one that is destined to survive. It is due to its giant pies that Denby Dale is well known throughout the United Kingdom and further afield. The people who arrive to live in the new estates are soon made aware of the village's history and certainly it is down to some of these individuals (alongside knowledgeable locals) that the pies of 1988 and 2000 were created. These people wanted to experience a Denby Dale pie first hand and in doing so became a part of the village's history and are to be congratulated for doing so.

So is a Denby Dale pie fun or folly? Local history and worthy cause or farce and fiasco? You are about to go on a journey to experience all of the above and, once completed, you must make up your own mind.

Historical Note:
I have tried to quote newspaper reports as a whole wherever possible, particularly with the older pies. People who actually attended the events created these reports. They experienced the day for themselves and created snapshots in time.

Chapter 1

1788

The Return to Sanity of King George III

Pie No. 1

Every so often the quiet, sleepy, village of Denby Dale loses its anonymity and achieves national and even worldwide attention. Every generation or so an enormous pie is baked, the earliest known tradition of which began over 200 years ago.

The first mention of a pie in the village is recorded in 1788, this date, though, seems to be slightly spurious. The reason for this is the event for which the pie was baked, the return to sanity of King George III (1738-1820). George, who had come to the throne of England in 1760, suffered a serious illness in 1765 and showed symptoms that were later linked to his 'madness' of 1788. This madness caused the king to foam at the mouth, talk incessantly for twenty-four hours at a time, scream sexual and other obscenities, and even engage in conversation with an oak tree, which he believed to be Frederick of Prussia. To combat this madness, the king was moved from Windsor to Kew in December where, by modern standards, he was treated horrendously. His mouth was gagged, burning poultices were applied to his body to drive away evil and he was strapped to a chair for hours. His madness, which later opinion has suggested was porphyria, a symptom of kidney disorder, which can poison the nervous system and, in extreme cases, the brain, passed and in April 1789 a service of thanksgiving was held at St Paul's Cathedral to celebrate his recovery. The king's troubles were well-recorded in the film *The Madness of King George* which starred the late Sir Nigel Hawthorne as George III.

Why did the people of Denby Dale see the king's recovery as a cause for a special celebration? As in 1765, his relapse in 1788 gave rise to a regency crisis, which led to the king's unpopular son, later George IV, taking temporary power. George's long reign was also a factor. In total he was king for almost sixty years and, like an old overcoat, his people were used to him.

George III. *(Courtesy of Roni Wilkinson.)*

He also connected with the common man and this was probably the clinching factor. He was dubbed 'Farmer George' by satirists, who at first mocked his interests in mundane matters and his homely thrift rather than politics. This was to contrast sharply with his son's extravagances and led to George being thought of as a man of the people. George III was also passionately interested in agriculture, particularly appropriate to the villagers of Denby Dale. Indeed, during his reign the agricultural revolution reached its zenith. The large growth in the rural population of England provided much of the workforce for the ideas conceived during his reign. When, by 1811, George entered his final descent into insanity, his personal popularity, though never inconsiderable, increased. It was now that his son became Prince Regent, a title he retained until his father's death in 1820.

In 1788 the manor of Denby was still in the hands of the Savile family and the court roll of 1787 includes the names of many families known to have lived in the hills around Dykeside at Denby and Ingbirchworth. Of the few people noted to be living at Dykeside we find Joseph Healey (two cottages), Benjamin Fretwell (cottage), John Lockwood (cottage) and Joshua Lockwood (cottage). Other names we find in Dykeside at this time were Horn, Schofield, Morley, Tyas, Hobson, Kilner and Moxon though there were others. Nathaniel Shirt ran the upper corn mill and the Wood family were becoming prominent in the area. Indeed the 1788 pie preceded the building of a new Wesleyan Methodist chapel in the village by only eleven years, this largely due to the religious zeal displayed by the brothers Joseph and John Wood. It is unlikely that we will ever know the names of the individuals responsible for the first recorded Denby Dale pie but we can at least be sure that some bearing the names mentioned above would certainly have taken part.

The date of the pie, though apparently not open to question, would appear to suggest that the Dalers were somewhat presumptive. In 1788 King George suffered a bilious attack, lapsed into insanity, and retired to Cheltenham on the advice of his doctors to partake of the healing properties of the spa waters there.

It seems possible that news of an improvement in the king's condition could have reached Denby Dykeside and that their elation caused them to bake a pie in celebration. As it turned out the king did not recover until the following year.

Leaving aside the year, very little is known about the beginning of this 200-year-old tradition.

A large game pie was cooked at the White Hart Inn, which may at this time have been known as the Joiner's Arms and was, more than likely, run by the Lockwood family. The pub was definitely known by the name of the White Hart by around 1840 and the same family continued

The king partaking of the spa waters.

to run it until at least 1889. Once ready, the pie was served to the villagers in Cliff Style Field across the road from the inn, close to the site where the later Victoria Memorial Hall was built in 1903.

The foundation for the baking of a large pie to celebrate local or national events was now begun, though it was to be another twenty-seven years before another one entered the annals of history.

A section of the OS Map of 1854, showing Cliff Style Field and the White Hart Inn.

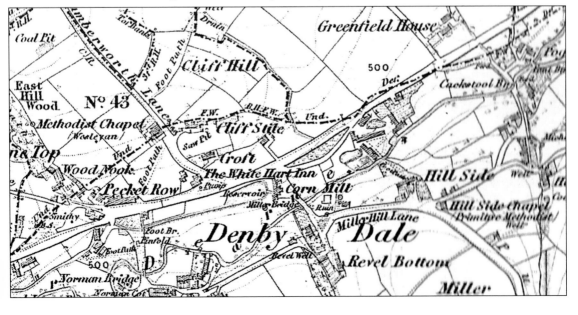

Chapter 2

1815

Wellington's Victory at Waterloo

Pie No. 2

By 1815 memories of Denby Dale's first pie had begun to fade. King George III was still nominally the monarch but in reality it was his son, George IV, the prince regent, who held power, his vices held in check as much as possible by the government of the day led by the Tory Robert Jenkinson, Second Earl of Liverpool.

In the early nineteenth century fears of a French invasion were paramount in the thoughts of England's population. Napoleon Boneparte, by virtue of his conquests in Europe, was threatening to march his armies across the channel and do what only William the Conqueror had managed to do: subdue and conquer England. Militia lists survive from Denby from 1806 detailing the names of the many volunteers who balanced the standing army and aided in local matters, not least was the fear of a French invasion.

It was no small sigh of relief that the country breathed when the Duke of Wellington defeated 'Boney' at Waterloo in 1815, thereby freeing the country from threat of invasion and establishing peace. The country rejoiced and the people of Denby Dale baked another pie to celebrate. The pie, by today's standards, was comparatively small containing:

Twenty fowls, two sheep and half a peck of flour for the crust.

The 'peck' unit of measurement has been in use since the fourteenth century and is most commonly known from the tongue twister: Peter Piper picked a peck of pickled peppers. In today's terms it is equal to 9.09 dry litres or 2 dry gallons.

The pie was the first to be baked in an oven built at the old corn mill, next to the River

(Courtesy of Roni Wilkinson.)

A nineteenth century cartoon depicting the victory at Waterloo.

A nineteenth century cartoon of the Duke of Wellington.

Dearne at the bottom of Miller Hill. In his book, *The Denby Dale Pies*, David Bostwick commented on the Denby Dale-based Waterloo veteran George Wilby, who was remembered to have hung his sword over the drawing room mantelpiece at his home, Pogstone House, Cuckstool, Denby Dale. Mr Bostwick noted that the triumphant return of this man could only have given impetus to the baking of this 'Victory' pie and that he may well have had the honour of carving the pie with his sword. It may also be that he set the precedent for subsequent ceremonial carvings for a specially commissioned knife and fork were used for all the later pies, the knife being cut to the shape of a sabre.

George Wilby (1797-1872) would have been eighteen years old at the time of the Battle of Waterloo. He married Harriet Elliott (1792-1841), with whom he had four children. The Wilby family remained at Pogstone House long after George, as did his sword, that was described as being:

> *About 2 feet 6 inches to 3 feet long blade, say 1½ inches wide and the handle had a protective curved guard over it.*

George Wilby (1797-1872), veteran of Waterloo and maybe the first man to make the first ceremonial cut into a Denby Dale pie.

The gravestone of George and Harriet Wilby, at Upper Denby Church.

Or an old mucky-looking thing according to others. The sword is now lost, George's great grandson Arthur Hinchliffe Wilby explained about this and the armour that went with it:

> *The information I have about the family history was first from my father (George Harold Wilby ,1872-1959), who told me that as a boy he used to play with the armour which [sic] had been handed down. His father (Arthur Ebenezer 1837-1902) was careless about such things and eventually it was destroyed or lost.*

In later life George Wilby was always described as 'Gentleman' and was recorded as a farmer of 30 acres and a registrar, he was also involved in local poor relief and the construction of the Woodhead Railway Tunnel on the Sheffield-to-Manchester line during the mid-nineteenth century.

We can never be sure that George Wilby did make the ceremonial first cut into this pie, but due to his connection with the Elliott family through his marriage to Harriet, we can be certain that he was involved in the next one.

Chapter 3

29 August 1846

The Repeal of the Corn Laws

Pie No. 3

As a result of the end of the Napoleonic wars an act was brought forward in 1815 by Prime Minister Robert Jenkinson to protect landed interest following the collapse of artificially high prices of corn and other cereals. During the wars British farmers had been encouraged to grow as much domestic produce as possible as imports from the continent were negligible and not guaranteed to continue. Now the wars were over these British farmers feared that imports from Europe would substantially reduce the price and therefore ruin them. This new act was an attempt to protect them until the price of British corn was eighty shillings a quarter. This was fine for the farmers but not so good for the poor. The result of the act was to keep the price of bread high, when bread was the staple diet of the poor.

The act became the symbol of the repression of the poor and found a unique voice in that of Ebenezer Elliott (1781-1849). From Rotherham, South Yorkshire, Elliott, who became known as the 'Corn Law Rhymer' wrote:

> Whoever does not oppose the Corn Law is a patron of want, national immorality, bankruptcy, child-murder, incendiary fires, midnight assassination and anarchy.

He became nationally established as a social critic in 1831 after the publication of his *Corn Law Rhymes*, which attacked the bread tax. He founded the first anti Corn Law society in England in 1830 and was a supporter of the Anti Corn Law League. This was headed by the Liberal MPs Cobden and Bright and yet for all the political agitation he and they caused, the act was not repealed until 1846 by Peel's outgoing government.

Ebenezer Elliott married his cousin Fanny Gartside and had at least thirteen children. From 1821 to 1842 he ran his own iron and steel business in Sheffield. He died in 1849, three years after seeing the abolition of the Corn Laws. His younger sister Harriet (1792-1841) had

Cobden, Peel and Bright, the MPs who headed the Anti Corn Law League.
(Courtesy of Roni Wilkinson.)

Ebenezer Elliott, the 'Corn Law Rhymer' (1781-1849).

(Courtesy of Roni Wilkinson.)

Richard Cobden (1804-1865).

Cover of the Anti Corn Law League membership document.

originally married William Booth Gartside (her cousin and brother to Fanny). The Gartside family, including Fanny and William Booth, were baptised at Cumberworth Church to Benjamin Gartside and Mary Green. Ebenezer's mother was Nancy (Ann) Gartside, who married Ebenezer Elliott senior. Evidently the two families had very close ties and Ebenezer would have been acquainted with Cumberworth and Denby Dale. After Harriet Elliott's husband William Booth Gartside died young she re-married, sometime before 1828, to a man we have already met, Waterloo veteran George Wilby, a man she must have got to know through her connections with Cumberworth. They had four children, the fourth, in 1837 being named Arthur Ebenezer in honour of her well known brother, a man who was later to be heavily involved in organising the next Denby Dale pie. The family home was made at Pogstone House at Cuckstool, Denby Dale, reputedly built by George but more likely this was a rebuild as we know that a property of that name on that site existed in 1731 and was occupied by Francis Burdett. The house was situated very close to Cuckstool Farm, which was also a part of the estate of George Wilby.

Thirty-one years of hardship for the poorer classes had ended and Denby Dale celebrated by baking their third recorded pie.

This pie was probably the most important in community terms, actually celebrating something that directly and adversely affected the people of the village. It was also the first real 'monster' pie. A village poet recorded the event in rhyme:

> *The rabbits will have to rue, for if they show a tail,*
> *They'll be shot and in the pot, be eat at Denby Dale*

Ebenezer Elliott would not have been oblivious to the event due to his sister's marriage to George Wilby and it would appear that the pie was baked close to where the couple lived. It could even have been that Elliott's relationship with his brother-in-law had been one of the reasons behind the celebrations. Living at Denby Dale was the sister of the Corn Law Rhymer and now that the hated bread tax was abolished, what was more natural than resurrecting a tradition last celebrated in 1815 when a veteran of Waterloo had returned home? Was Elliott in the crowd that day? With his brother-in-law? We may never know, his name is not recorded by anybody contemporary, though it is inconceivable that Denby Dale gentleman farmer George Wilby, along with his wife Harriet Elliott, were not present.

Family tree showing the union of the Elliott and Wilby families.

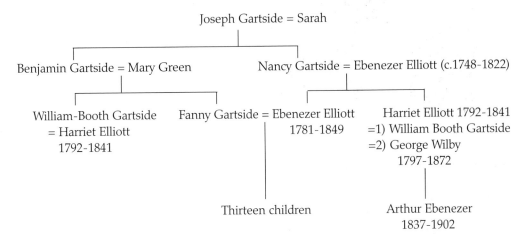

Oral tradition remembered that a building in front of Cuckstool farmhouse, which served as a dye house and plasterers workshop, was used to house the oven and bake the 1846 pie. This was to be the last of the stand-alone pies. As they grew bigger a dish was to be required for future bakes. This is not to say that the 1846 pie was small, far from it. The large pastry container was 21 feet in circumference and 1 foot 10 inches deep, and was used to contain the following mind-boggling list of ingredients:

44¹/₂ stones of flour, 19lbs of lard, 16lbs of butter, 7 hares, 14 rabbits, 4 pheasants, 4 grouse, 2 ducks, 2 geese, 2 turkeys, 2 guinea fowls, 4 hens, 6 pigeons, 63 small birds, 5 sheep, 1 calf and 100lbs of beef.

The pie dish was lined with pastry, into which the whole of the above was placed and covered with a pastry top. After ten-and-a-half hours of baking, it was pronounced cooked, removed from the oven and put onto a dray to be towed from Cuckstool to Norman Park to the accompaniment of three bands. Finally, the procession complete, the pie was put onto a temporary stage in front of a fast-growing crowd of people.

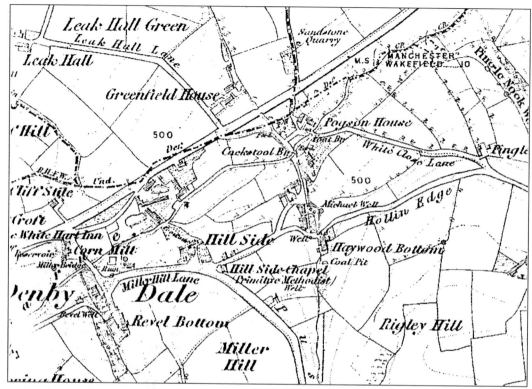

A section of the OS map of 1854, showing the location of Cuckstool and Pogs(t)on(e) House.

The following report in the *Barnsley Chronicle*, dated 19 March 1887, recaps the story and reports on subsequent events:

The Denby Dale Pie

W North of Gomersall, in a Leeds contemporary, gives the following description of the Denby Dale Pie of 1846 as told him by a 'native'.

'At Doyke Soide they loiken poie' is now something more than a local saying; but very few people, I should imagine, are aware how, where and when it originated. At the time (1860) I first made the acquaintance of the district, I had scarce lived long enough to get rid of my first set of teeth, and the baking of the pie, as told by one of its cooks, formed one of the 2001 tales of the village. The 'scheherazade' of those days, unlike the one we have read of, was an old dame dressed in a bed gown, and wearing a mob cap; and, if my antiquarian tastes had then been as keen as they are now, much interesting information might have been acquired.

The following particulars relating to the contents of the pie, although from good authority, are not given as absolutely accurate, but more with the object of showing that there are more recipes than one as to what it consisted of:- Flour 44½ stone, Suet 91½ lbs., Lard 19lb, Fresh

Butter 16lb, Beef 100lb, one calf, five sheep, seven hares, fourteen rabbits, four pheasants, four partridges, two brace of grouse, six pigeons, two turkeys, two guinea fowls, four ducks, four geese, four fowls, 63 small birds and 1lb of pepper. The circumference of the pie was 21 feet and its height or depth 2 feet 3 inches. The crust was prepared by three or four of the best cooks in the neighbourhood and the whole placed in a specially prepared oven on the estate of Mr G Wilby.

When the pie was baked, its removal and subsequent division was made the occasion of a general holiday it being drawn on a lorry amid much rejoicing to a large pie field then in the occupation of the late Mr James Peace of Inkerman Hall, about midway between Denby Dale and Upper Denby. I cannot call to mind now who was the fortunate individual delegated to do the carving but I should imagine it would be Mr James Peace, from the fact that the knife and fork used on that occasion were, when I last saw them, in the possession of that gentleman. The knife, I should think, would be a yard in length and the fork of a proportionate size. In later years I used to pass through that memorable field on my way to the Rev Job Johnson's school at Upper Denby, and have often had my attention drawn to the spot where the pie was cut up; for the grass over a considerable area was of a deeper and darker tint, particularly in the spring time. But considering the time about which I write would be nearly twenty years subsequent to the baking of the pie, the probabilities are that it might be caused by a defective drain from the farm, situated at a higher elevation on the margin of the field. Fragments of the pie were carefully preserved by some of the recipients for many years. One, I know, had a small cabinet made, in which was kept a portion of the suet crust; and one day, I well remember, I was given a small, flint like piece as a great favour in order that I might say that I had tasted the veritable pie. My knowledge of the oven in which the pie was baked is much more authentic, for I have played (laiked – we called it) in it times out of mind. Built on the edge of a tributary of the River Don, and within a stone's throw (almost) of the Woodhead and Wakefield turnpike road, it would strike the passer-by as being but an insignificant outhouse to one of the cottages adjacent; and such it really was, for a few years prior to the time of which I write, it had been converted into the warehouse of a painter and plasterer. Past one corner of it was a narrow wooden bridge, other traffic having to ford through the water below. It is now many years since I was last in that neighbourhood; but I believe the oven is still in existence and put to the same use. Mr John Wood, of Penistone, commenting on the same last week says: 'I venture to ask if more than one great pie was made at Denby Dale in the year of 1846 to celebrate the repeal of the Corn Laws.' I attended at the celebration of this event in 1846. A temporary stage had been erected and a large number of people assembled in a field on or adjoining the north side of the Dale. Near the north east corner of this field stands the Denby Dale Wesleyan Chapel. An immense pie was brought into this field on a farmer's wagon and lifted onto the temporary stage. Some speeches were then made and as the crowd below increased, so did the people on the stage, until, whilst one of the orators was holding forth on the advantages of a cheap loaf, the stage gave way and came down, pie and all with a crash. A crowd of 15,000 people surged forward, a scramble ensued and amid a wild state of turmoil and riot the stage was utterly demolished and the pie flung to the winds. There was no formal cutting up; some rough fellows took possession of it and in their struggles to obtain a share actually waded ankle-deep in the meat and gravy. The celebration came to a sudden end. Some names were taken down and a prosecution took place before the magistrates at Barnsley. Calling in at the New Inn at Denby, on my way to Penistone, I obtained a piece of the pie, which I thought was very good, from 'New John' of Ingbirchworth'.

Another version of the disastrous day's proceedings suggests that it was a Tory plot to ruin the largely Liberal celebrations and that certain men were bribed to vandalise the platform. That it was a politically motivated act of sabotage seems to gain authenticity when one considers a letter written by a Mr Jonas France of Middlesbrough, who disclosed the truth to the *Huddersfield Examiner* some years later:

> *I think that you will get information about the pie coming to grief before it got served out through the Tories getting all the navvies they could together and walking them about half drunk. At a given signal they were to rush at the wagon the pie was on and trample it to pieces, which they did.*

Jonas France had worked in the Wakefield and, evidently, the Denby Dale area as a bricklayer. He added that he and another labourer had built the oven at Cuckstool.

> *We built the oven for a railway 'tommy' (bread) shop, as the Huddersfield and Penistone line was just beginning to be made. The oven was 12 feet by 11 feet and the back end of it was pulled out to allow the pie to be run in on a dray of some kind.*

Forty-year-old Mr James Peace (1806-1885), who lived at Inkerman Hall and was the founder of Inkerman Mill on the Barnsley Road in Denby Dale, should have had the honour of cutting the pie but was denied the chance. James Peace married Narah Horton and amongst his eleven children were Ellen Peace who married Joseph Henry Dewhirst, and Hannah Horton Peace who married Denby Dale mill owner Zaccheus Hinchliffe, though both marriages were made after the 1846 pie celebrations.

A special knife and fork had been obtained for the event, possibly influenced by George Wilby's sabre in 1815, thereby setting the precedent for future occasions. According to another tradition, Mr Peace made such a lengthy speech that two men from Clayton West grew bored and knocked out some of the platform supports, the stage collapsed and Mr Peace fell into the pie. It was suggested at the time that this could also have been an act of sabotage by the villagers of Clayton West.

Earlier the same day the people of Clayton baked a 16 stone pudding, which contained 240lbs of flour, 20lbs of suet and 100lbs of currants. As with the Denby Dale pie it was baked to celebrate the Repeal of the Corn Laws, though it did not compare in size with the Denby Dale monster and was satirised in a poem written at the time, in the final verse:

Believed to be James Peace (1806-1885), of Inkerman House. The man who fell into the 1846 pie.

Come all ye lads of Denby Dale
And listen to me awhile;
A tale so true I'll tell to you
Twill cause you all to smile.

In 1846 they resolved to have a meal
And drink the health of three great men,
Cobden, Bright and Peel.

They made a thumping pie my boys,
Such a one you never saw;
It took eight horses large and strong
From the oven it to draw.

You poachers of the countryside
May each lay down his gun,
For pheasants, partridges and ground game,
We've killed them every one.

The rabbits too will have to rue,
For if they show a tail,
They'll all be shot and in the pot
Be eat at Denby Dale.

The pigeons, too, will all get killed
If they don't quickly fly;
For they must also do their share
In filling this great pie.

At Clayton West, they did their best,
A pudding they had made;
But Denby Dale made them turn pale,
When rejoicing at Free Trade.

Perhaps certain members of the Clayton West community did not relish the thought of being outdone by their near neighbours.

It is clear from the above that there were numerous stories concerning the abrupt termination of the day's proceedings, possibly emanating from the confusion caused in the ensuing riot. But whether people from Clayton West were involved or not, they certainly had their noses in front of the Denby Dalers that year.

Chapter 4

27 August 1887

Queen Victoria's Golden Jubilee
Pie No. 4

In 1887 Victoria's Golden Jubilee was a national celebration of her 50th year as Queen. The Golden Jubilee brought her out of the shell she had been hiding in since the death of her husband and consort Prince Albert, and she once again embraced public life. She toured English possessions and even visited France (the first English monarch to do so since the coronation of Henry VI in 1431).

Victoria's long reign witnessed an evolution in English politics and the expansion of the British Empire, as well as political and social reforms on the continent. France had known two dynasties and embraced Republicanism, Spain had seen three monarchs and both Italy and Germany had united their separate principalities into national coalitions. Even in her dotage, she maintained a youthful energy and optimism that infected the English population as a whole. National pride was connected with the name of Victoria. The term Victorian England for example, stemmed from the queen's ethics and personal tastes, which generally reflected those of the middle class.

Queen Victoria's golden jubilee finally caused the people of Denby Dale to risk baking a fourth giant pie. Forty-one years had passed since the fiasco of 1846 and a new generation was yet to experience such an occasion, but there must have been a few nerves jangling as the decision was taken. The village itself had changed enormously in the intervening years due to the arrival of the railway.

Building work began on the first wooden viaduct in 1845, it was damaged by a storm in the winter of 1847 whilst still under construction, but the line finally opened on 1 July 1850. The wooden viaduct was eventually replaced by a more permanent stone structure and this was officially opened in 1880. Travel and trade opportunities opened up new worlds to the villagers and to the industries that had settled in the valley. Home-based handloom weaving had gradually given way as mechanisation took over and the mills began to tempt a ready supply of skilled workers into their factories. Three major ones sprang up in Denby Dale: Z Hinchliffe & Sons in 1850; Jonas Kenyon & Sons in 1854; and Brownhill and Scatchard in 1868 – all identifying a skilled and available labour source alongside the power to be derived from the River Dearne. The Naylor's and Joe Kitson's groups began manufacturing earthenware pipes and bricks as the opportunities to reach more distant markets opened up, indeed the Naylor's group grew in Denby Dale after being given the contract to build the stone viaduct in 1877. New housing was needed to supply the large influx of people moving to the village seeking work as the demand increased, and so the size of the village and its population grew accordingly.

A committee was formed to oversee affairs and it was decided that this pie should be larger than any before and that the funds for it should be raised by public subscription. It was also decided that the people of Denby Dale, children and the old aged should get a share first, before allowing the general public its opportunity. The Committee designed fund raising ventures, that would hopefully cover the cost of staging the event and with luck leave a little over to be used for local charities. Sixpence each was charged for viewing the pie. A funfair and refreshments were organised and plates were commissioned for sale, these bore a portrait of Queen Victoria and the relevant dates and sizes relating to the day. Special train services were to run from Bradford, Dewsbury and Halifax, the simple village feast had now moved on a stage and was expected to pull in crowds from much further afield. For the first time the pie was to remain in a dish, thereby dispelling fears of any possible repetition of the 1846 proceedings. Prior to this the pies had been 'stand pies', similar in looks to huge pork pies, with only the pastry sides and crust holding it together.

The contract to make the dish was originally given to Joseph Barraclough, the blacksmith of Upper Denby, but he sub-let it to W C Holmes & Co of Huddersfield who were more notable for making gasometers. Weighing 15cwt, it was 8 feet in diameter and 2 feet deep and made from riveted sheet steel and angle iron, it was to be the biggest pie so far. A special oven was designed and built by Jonas Drake & Sons of Halifax behind the White Hart Inn. It consisted of 3,000 red bricks, 5,000 firebricks, 50 enamelled bricks and 30cwt of fireclay, all of which were supplied by Kitson's Brick and Tile Company, Denby Dale. This huge oven, which was 14 feet square on the outside and 10 feet square on the inside, was fitted with a flue so as to equalise the heat in all parts of the pie and took five men ten days to build. A stewing boiler adjoined the oven, this was made by Joseph Barraclough, it held 80 gallons and the meat was stewed in here before being placed in the pie.

The Pie Committee decided to employ a company from Halifax to undertake the actual baking process. The firm of F Workman & Sons was chosen for this task and even though they were professional bakers they would never have overseen anything like this before. The ingredients alone should have been enough to put them off:

1581lbs of beef, 163lbs of veal, 180lbs of lamb, 180lbs of mutton, 250lbs of lean pork, 40 pigeons, 42 fowls, 3 hares, 64 rabbits, 12 grouse, 21 ducks, 4 plovers, 1 turkey, 5 geese, 2 wild ducks, 108 small birds, 20lbs of suet and 42 stones of potatoes.

The professional bakers hired a London chef for the project, though on the night before the big day this man caught a train back to the capital, it was a warning.

The *Barnsley Chronicle* reported on the preparations on 27 August 1887:

> *Denby Dale is to distinguish itself today by the production of another pie. The occasion being the local celebration of the Queen's Jubilee. This pie, which is the result of a public subscription, will be 8 feet diameter and 2 feet deep. A very large brick oven has been built, and during the week has been tested frequently. The first trial was made with some bread, and the result was considered satisfactory. The first loaf brought out was presented to Mr A E Wilby, who is working very hard towards making the celebration a success. The dish, which has been specially cast for the occasion, is made of iron, and altogether the necessary arrangements for baking &c., have cost £100.*

Arthur Ebenezer Wilby (1837-1902).

Here we find Arthur Ebenezer Wilby noted to be very involved with proceedings. It is tempting to speculate that he may have seen this as a family responsibility, thereby giving greater weight to his father's involvement in previous years. As we have noted earlier, George Wilby, the Waterloo veteran, may have been involved in 1815 and was almost certainly a patron in 1846. Though George had died in 1872, Arthur Ebenezer would have been well aware of the truth of the matter and I believe his support for the venture speaks for itself.

The *Barnsley Chronicle* continues:

> *We English people would scarcely call ourselves a nation of gourmands, nor would we admit that the science of eating has yet become the study of a very large portion of our population. Perhaps if our eating were more scientific it would not be any the worse, but rather much better for our general health. Be that as it may, we do not yet make cooking our chief study, but we have a fondness for good living and from early times have been accustomed to use the table as the most fitting means of honouring men and events . . .*
>
> *The preparations – the question, what kind of pie shall it be? had to be considered. At the celebration of the Repeal of the Corn Laws a raised pie was made, which, with the fall of the platform, was knocked to pieces. It was resolved that the jubilee pie should be baked in a dish so that there would be no fear of it meeting with a fate like that of its predecessor.*
>
> *The greater part of the material of which the pie was made was exhibited for a day or two previously to the making at the shop of Mr Mathews, a local butcher.*

We must here remember to consider that it was the middle of summer, the meat was then cut up and cooked in the boiler in batches before being transferred to the pie dish. Freshly cooked and hot meat and gravy was then added to that which had already been deposited into the dish,

Programme for the Day,

AUGUST 27th, 1887.

11-30—The PIE leaves the White Hart, drawn by 20 horses, for NORMAN PARK.

Four Prizes are given to the Owners of BEST GROOMED AND DECORATED HORSES, viz., 10/-, 7/6, 5/-, 2/6.

1-0—The Gates are opened for Admission, 6d. each.

1 to 3-30—The Pie is on View in front of Marquee.

3-0—PROCESSION from White Hart of Band, Children, &c.

3-30—HENRY J. BRIERLEY, Esq., Denby Dale, will cut into the Pie.

3-30 to 4-10—Serving of Pie to Aged, Children, and Subscribers.

4.10 to 5.10—Serving of Pie to Inhabitants of Parishes of Denby Dale and Cumberworth.

5.10—Serving of Pie to General Public.

4.15—JUVENILE SPORTS.

SACK RACE, 80 yards. Prize, Cricket Bat value 10/-

THREE-LEGGED RACE, 100 yards. Prize, one dozen Pie Plates value 6/-

OBSTACLE RACE, 120 yards. Prize, Cricket Bat value 10/-

FOR GIRLS ONLY—SKIPPING MATCH—Prize, Electro-plated Teapot value 15/-

4.45—DONKEY RACE, 400 yards. Prize, New Bridle. Entrance Free.

DENBY DALE PIE.

THIS romantic and enterprising village has always been renowned for its Pies. Its history in this respect being without an equal in the annals of the whole world.

The first Pie was baked in 1788, in commemoration of King George III's recovery from his terrible mental affliction, the recovery being marked by universal rejoicing throughout England. The Pie was baked in a field called Cliffe Style Field, just behind the White Hart Inn.

The Second Pie was made in 1815, in honour of the great peace which was ratified after the Battle of Waterloo and defeat and downfall of Napoleon I.

Its contents were, half a sheep, 20 fowls, and half a pack of flour. The Pie was baked in the kiln attached to the Denby Dale Corn Mill

The Third Pie was in commemoration of the Repeal of the Corn Laws, and was held on August 19th, 1846.

Its contents were 44½ stones flour, 9¼lbs. suet, 19lbs. lard, 16lbs. butter, 7 hares, 14 rabbits, 2 brace pheasants, 2 brace partridges, 2 brace grouse, couple ducks, couple geese, pair turkeys, pair guinea fowls, 2 pairs common fowls, 6 pigeons, 63 small birds, 5 sheep, 1 calf, and 100lbs. beef.

This pie was baked in a bakery at Cuck Stool, or the Ducking Stool, Denby Dale. It was successfully baked, and put on to a platform to be cut up and served. However, the platform gave way, precipitating the pie on to the ground. A crowd of 15,000 people surged forward, a scramble ensued, and amid a wild state of turmoil and riot the stage was utterly demolished and the pie flung to the winds.

The Fourth and present Pie is in honour of the Jubilee of our gracious Queen Victoria, and further to shew the world we are true to the traditions of our forefathers.

The oven is designed and built by Messrs. Jonas Drake & Sons, Halifax, and was completed in ten days by five men. It is 14 feet square outside, and ten feet square within, fitted and contrived to equalise the heat in all parts, and situated near the White Hart Inn. The bricks were supplied by Mr. Joe Kitson, Denby Dale. The oven contains 3000 red bricks, 5000 fire bricks, and 500 enamelled faced bricks, and 30 cwt of fire clay.

The boiler adjoining, to stew the meat, is capable of holding 80 gallons, and is supplied by Mr. Joseph Barraclough, Denby.

The dish is made of sheet and angle iron, rivetted together, weighing 15 cwt, and is made by Messrs. W. C. Holmes & Co., Huddersfield.

The size of this pie is 8 feet in diameter, and 2 feet deep, and the baker is Mr. F. Workman, Halifax.

The Knife is 30 inches long, and the Fork two feet long.

The Contents of the Pie are: Flour 60 stones, beef 850 lbs., mutton 160 lbs., veal 160 lbs., lamb 250 lbs., lean pork 250 lbs., lard 100 lbs., butter 50 lbs., rabbits 32, hares 3, fowls 52, pigeons 40, grouse 12, ducks 6, plovers 4, turkey 1, geese 5, small birds 100.

The whole contents weigh about 200 stones, or 1 ton, 5 cwt

COMMITTEES.

CUTTING UP THE PIE—Messrs. J. H. Dewhirst, T. D. Matthews, Walter Holmes, and W. Lister.

SERVING THE PIE—No. 1 TABLE—Messrs. John Brierley, John Hinchliffe, J. P. Hinchliffe, J. W. Brierley, and Thomas Hinchliffe.

Waiters—Tom Barraclough and H. Liversedge.

No. 2 TABLE—Messrs. M. Worsley, H. Kitson, Thos. Hirst, Abel Barraclough, Allen Brownhill, W. Walker.

Waiters—Geo. H. Schofield and Joe Kitson.

No. 3 TABLE—Messrs. Thos. Lake, Geo. Broadhead, J. W. Spivey, Arthy Peace, James Peace, and Geo. Dyson.

Waiters—Sam Barraclough and A. Kitson.

No. 4 TABLE—Messrs. A. E. Wilby, W. Child, W. Hargreaves, A. Matthews, W. Crosland, Joseph Blacker.

Waiters—John Parker and A. Dalton.

SIDEBOARD WAITERS—F. Dearnley, H. Hanson, Evan McDonald, W. A. Heap, James Thewlis, John Lockwood, W. Castle.

SPORTS COMMITTEE—Messrs. Thos. Ineson, Edward Kitson, A. Lockwood, Henry Hirst, Smith Kenyon, Allen Lockwood, Sam Lockwood, Luke Marsden.

TICKET COMMITTEE—SELLING—Messrs. G. H. Green, C. W. Haigh.

COLLECTING AT GATE—Messrs. James Turton, Walter Hirst, Alfred Hanson, C. K. Hanwell.

AT MARQUEE—John McDonald, Willie Spivey, John Boothroyd, Joe Heywood, Harry Whiteley, Squire Senior.

PROGRAMMES—Messrs. Fred Brierley, A. Beever.

PLATE SELLING—Messrs. W. Howard, L. W. Ellis.

PRESTON BROS. & CO., PRINTERS, HUDDERSFIELD.

PROGRAMME Continued.

4-55—TUG OF WAR. Prize, One Guinea. Entrance 1/- each.

6-0—GRAND GALA, accompanied by the DENBY DALE BRASS BAND.

Professor JAMES' PUNCH & JUDY

Will perform at 2-30 p.m., 3-30 p.m., 4-30 p.m., and 5-30 p.m.

One o'clock to Dusk.

JUBILEE JENNY SLIDE.

Grand Display of Fireworks

At 8 p.m., by J. W. Potter, Dalton, Huddersfield.

Refreshments on the Ground.

REFRESHMENT CATERERS:

Messrs. SMART & TOWNEND,

Wren's Hotel, New Briggate, Leeds.

The Committee reserve the right to alter the Programme, if necessary.

Pass Out Checks after 4-30.

lying there going cold. Placed in layers around the inside edge of the dish were game birds that were meant to cook when the pie finally entered the oven. The 42 stones of potatoes were then added to the mixture, on top of this were placed earthenware bowls full of gravy in order to try to fill up the huge dish and to help support the crust, which was already laying on a reinforcing layer of canvas. With its crust and including the dish the pie weighed nearly 1½ tons. Just before midnight on Thursday 25 August, the pie entered the oven where it remained until ten o'clock on Friday when it was removed and placed in an outhouse to cool before the big day. Although the pie was reported to be 'done to a turn', Mr Workman left the village on Friday night never to be seen again. He knew what the committee, the villagers and the tourists would find out the following day.

The *Barnsley Chronicle* continues:

The celebration was fixed for Saturday last and, in view of the attraction, the Lancashire and Yorkshire and Manchester, Sheffield and Lincolnshire Railway companies afforded special facilities for visiting Denby Dale. Single fairs for the double journey were allowed from all parts where the single fair was more than 9d. The arrangements were that the pie should be drawn from the White Hart Inn to Norman Park, where the demonstration should take place, and the pie, being cut into by Mr Henry J Brierley, should be served first to the aged people and school children, then to the subscribers and last to the general public. It was also intended that there should be sports and a gala, with dancing to the music of the Denby Dale Brass Band. But 'the best laid schemes of mice and men gang aft aglee'.

All the preparations were made, as we have said, and punctually to the time appointed, the pie-decorated with flowers was drawn from the White Hart Inn, through the village to Norman Park, close by Inkerman Hall, by nine horses, the committee following in precession. A large marquee had been erected and fitted with seats and tables, which were nicely decorated with flowers and plants for the feast. In front of the marquee the pie was placed, and further decorated with flowers, and the knife, 2 feet 6 inches long and the fork, 2 feet long, with which Mr Henry J Brierley was to cut the pie, were suspended near it. It was then photographed by Mr Duffus of Huddersfield. The committee were also photographed and everything seemed to be in readiness for properly utilising the mass of provision in the pie for the refection of those for whom it was intended, the committee having their places allotted to them as follows:

Cutting up the pie: Messrs J H Dewhirst, T D Mathews, Walter Holmes and W Lister.

Serving the pie: No 1 table John Brierley, John Hinchliffe, J P Hinchliffe, J W Brierley and Thomas Hinchliffe; waiters Tom Barraclough and H Liversedge. No 2 table M Worsley, H Kitson, Thomas Hirst, Abel Barraclough, Allen Brownhill and W Walker, waiters George H Schofield and H Kitson. No 3 table Thomas Lake, George Broadhead, J W Spivey, Arthy Peace, James Peace and Geo. Dyson, waiters Sam Barraclough and A Kitson. No 4 table A E Wilby, W Child, W Hargreaves, A Mathews, W Crossland and Jos Blacker, waiters John Parker and A Dalton.

Sideboard waiters: F Dearnley, H Hanson, Evan McDonald, W A Heap, J Thewlis, J Lockwood, W Castle, J Hardy and A Castle.

Sports committee: Thomas Ineson, Edward Kitson, A Lockwood, Henry Hirst, Smith Kenyon, Allen Lockwood, Sam Lockwood and Luke Marsden.

Ticket committee: Selling – G H Green and C W Haigh; collecting at gate James Turton, Walter Hirst, Alfred Hanson and C K Hanwell; at Marquee – John McDonald, Willie Spivey, John Boothroyd, Joe Heywood, Harry Whitely and Squire Senior.

Decoration committee: Misses E Smithson, A Smithson, R Smithson, J Smithson. Miss Wood, Miss H A Wood, Mrs Workman and Miss Horne.

Programmes: Fred Brierley and A Beever.

Plate selling: W Howard and L W Ellis.

Many thousands of people swarmed into the village intent on having a good time and, of course, a piece of the giant pie. The programme of the day's events promised that the pie would be on view from 1.00pm to 3.30pm in Norman Park and that when the locals, children and the old had been served, the general public were to have their share, although those without a

The 1887 pie, covered by a white tarpaulin, just after being drawn from the oven at the corn mill behind it, surrounded by members of the committee. *(The National Archives.)*

The pie on display in Norman Park surrounded by an expectant public. *(The National Archives.)*

The 1887 Pie Committee photographed in Norman Park, prior to the opening of the pie. *(The National Archives.)*

A panorama depicting the pie celebrations at Denby Dale in 1887 in full swing. Note Inkerman Mill on the skyline and the marquees in Norman Park. Cottages on Hillside and Springfield Mill can be seen to the bottom right just below the busy Wakefield Road. The solitary building on Wakefield Road still survives, formerly Marsden's Hardware, it is now part of the Hair & Beauty Studio. (*Susan Buckley collection.*)

programme would have been unaware of these arrangements as they were never publicly announced. The mass of visitors began to cause a crush around the barriers surrounding the marquee, so much so that the procession of 700 schoolchildren lead by Denby Dale Brass Band struggled to reach the enclosure as people held onto to their vantage points with grim determination. People were already beginning to sneak into the tent, the flower trimmings on the pie were hastily grabbed whilst the carvers took their positions, waiting for the 3.30pm deadline for cutting the pie. The chairman of the committee, Mr Henry Josiah Brierley, had been given this honour, but no sooner had he stood to make his speech than the crowd surged forward clamouring for a piece of the pie.

The *Barnsley Chronicle* headline:

3 September 1887, Denby Dale Pie, A Unique Jubilee Celebration, Disgraceful Scenes

In opening the pie Mr H J Brierley had intended to say –

'Ladies and Gentlemen. We are met today to celebrate our queen's jubilee in a manner which we hope will give you a days enjoyment and innocent amusement to you all . . . we in Denby Dale have a weakness for pies. Antiquity can well attest the fact, our fathers had in 1846, our grandfathers in 1815 and our great grandfathers had in 1788.'

Henry Josiah Brierley (1863-1909), the man who was supposed to open the 1887 pie.

The speech, however, was not delivered, for the crowd within the enclosure increased so rapidly, and it became so evident that all discipline would soon be cast to the winds, that, the carvers being in their places, and in the absence of H J Brierley, Mr John Brierley took up the special knife and fork, and turning to the crowd began, 'Ladies and Gentlemen, we hail you with right good cheer on this occasion.' He got no further, however, for at that moment the barricade gave way and the crowd rushed into the enclosure and surrounded the pie. Plunging his knife quickly into the pie Mr Brierley and the other carvers quickly filled a number of dishes, and before they were absolutely surrounded succeeded in sending a supply to the old people and children already seated. This accomplished, the committee, though they strained every nerve, were utterly unable to carry out the programme further. Those who were in front of the crowd on reaching the wagon stopped, and the committee, under great excitement, tried to keep them back. But Mrs Partington's attempt to sweep back the Atlantic with a broom was not more hopeless than the efforts of the few committee men to repel the surging noisy crowd. For a minute or two they were restrained and then from every side, shouting 'Give's a bit o' poie', 'Let's have a bit o' crust', they swarmed round the carvers, pressing upon them, and one or two reaching on to the pie tried to snatch pieces from the dish. It was in vain Mr Brierley adjured them, 'If you are

Englishmen, stand back', and equally in vain that some of the carvers brandished their knives. A few police officers struggled in the throng, and were for a time swayed hither and thither like corks on the surface of a flood. The pie, when cut into, proved to be somewhat high and gamey, and its odour proved quite sufficient for some, and very few managed to make a meal of it. But the struggle for a 'bit of the crust' went on vigorously, and the carvers were many a time forced into self-defence to hand pieces to those nearest them. Mr Supt Kane and Inspector Calcraft were in charge of the police, a force of eighteen men being on the ground; and, massing most of those about the pie, vigorous measures thinned the mob, for such it had become, for a few minutes but it quickly closed in again. One vigorous member of the committee mounted the sideboard, and wielding his stick vigorously, for a time rendered it possible to hand dishes over into the marquee. But the crowd flocked into the marquee, where the scene of struggling and shouting was repeated, and a great amount of waste was caused. For an hour the disgraceful scene continued, dishes and buckets in which the pie was placed to be handed to the people in the marquee being unceremoniously robbed of the pieces of crust they contained, a dozen hands grabbing at every morsel which appeared. Not until Mr Brierley announced that when the old people had been served the pie would be conveyed into the open field was there any cessation of the struggle, but then most of the crust had been taken. In the last quarter of an hour in which the pie was in the tent many women pressed forward to get a look at it, and caustic indeed were their remarks at what they saw, the wreck and disorder the disorderly crowd had created. About half past four o'clock the pie was wheeled out into the open field, where it was left, and very soon afterwards the dish was surrounded by lads and young men, who with pocket knives cut off pieces of crust or sought out the bones, of which a very few had found their way into the pie, and threw them about amongst their companions and bystanders, some of whom took them away as relics.

Another fiasco had unfolded in Denby Dale. People trying to break off pieces of crust as souvenirs, and the once-eager patrons then melting back as the most nauseating stench began to fill the atmosphere. The 20 foot birth given to the offending object would seem to have implied that the pie was thoroughly rotten. To a bystander the comic about turn by the once eager people, for whom by now just a sniff of the pie was enough, must have been mellowed by the thoughts of the officials and the police in as much as that serious injury had probably been avoided. One local man, Benny Beever, a young lad at the time but later a well-known local character we shall meet again, swore that a neighbouring pack of foxhounds hunted the smell from 5 miles away.

The once majestic record breaker now sat in melancholy embarrassment, its crust ripped to shreds and its trimmings gone. The crowds had begun to melt away and the day was effectively over and ruined. The accounts told a sorry tale:

Hire of marquee and small tent	£ 19 17s 6d
Damaged to same	£ 14 3s 1½d

Evidently the cooking procedure had been at fault and reports of a brace of 'gamey' grouse and what looked to be a skinned fox can't have helped matters. The crowds must have suffered mixed emotions, probably ranging from hilarity and bewilderment to a sense of feeling cheated. A letter to the *Huddersfield Examiner* explains:

On the Wednesday previous to the pie day, the meat appeared to be alright with the exception of something which looked very like a skinned fox, and a brace of grouse which smelt very gamey. I think it was the process of cooking which made matters worse. The pan in which the meat was cooked was much too small and had to be refilled a large number of times; and every time the pan of hot victuals was emptied into the dish amongst that which had gone cold it helped to turn it sourer and sourer every time. What with the cooking and what with the ancient history of some of the meat previous to cooking and the pie dish standing in the sun all day long receiving its cargo it turned putrid, and on Thursday when the dish was only about half full it was condemned by some of the promoters. The next question was, how can the pie dish be filled with the least expense? (Remember they had received nearly all the stuff free of charge up to this time) and it was decided to fill up with potatoes, so from 30 to 40 stones of 'taties' were thrown in, some pared or scraped, others should have been; but still the pan was not full, and being tired of wasting good 'taties' after bad meat, they filled up with jars, bowls, waterpots, cans, pails, buckets and anything that came their way, and the cover of the pie was put on, and the stinking mess was placed in the oven to bake. A still tongue was to be kept; let the advertisement go forward that a grand procession would take place at three o'clock and the multitude will come to look and pay. The pie was taken into the field before dinner and the hosts of strangers who poured into Denby Dale last Saturday afternoon were charged 6d each to go into the field to look at it. The farce was kept up to the very end. I am astonished how the promoters of the scheme dare offer the pie for human food; the nuisance inspector was present and the police neglected their duty.

Further details of a somewhat blatant disregard of health and safety were supplied from Holmfirth:

It was rather hard on some of the Holmfirth guests who accepted on Saturday last the general invitation of the Denby Dale Pie Committee to join the 'spread' after being served out of the pie with a tasty bit in the shape of a fowl, to find that it had not been very well plucked, but worse still when they found it had not been drawn… they divided the carcass and resolved to keep their portions as Jubilee Pie mementoes. One of the party is the possessor of what would have been a newly laid egg.

The opinions of many of the crowd were reported thus:

There were many objurgatory observations made about the pie, which it would be profane to give and therefore we forbear. But we may say that there seemed to be in the minds of some of the people an idea that it was nothing but a swindle.

The remains of the pie made a final journey on Sunday 28 August. Nine horses pulled the cart holding the dish and its dubious contents in a funeral procession to a field near Toby Wood Farm (between Denby Dale and Upper Denby). Here the remnants of meat, potato and crust were emptied into a pit and buried in quick lime. Perhaps in poor taste, though a keen illustration of the general feeling of local embarrassment, a funeral card was printed, as was the tradition at the time when a loved one had passed away.

The funeral procession of what was left of the 1887 Denby Dale pie makes its sombre way towards the burial site at Toby Wood.

In Affectionate Remembrance of the Denby Dale Pie, which died 27 August 1887, aged three days.

The verse read as follows:

> *Strong was the smell that compelled us to part,*
> *From a treat to our stomach and a salve to our heart;*
> *Like the last Denby Dale Pie which the crowd did assail,*
> *Its contents a rank mixture, it quickly turned stale;*
> *Though we could not eat, yet we still lingered near,*
> *Till the stench proved too much for a nassals to bear;*
> *So like sensible men the committee did say:*
> *'Twas better to inter it without further delay.*

The fourth Denby Dale pie had ended in disaster, and it was the second one on the trot, though it would appear that at least some portions of this one were actually eaten. It had cost £190 to stage according to the balance sheet.

The final details of the day's events were reported in the *Barnsley Chronicle*:

The knife and fork with which the pie was first cut were made for the purpose by Messrs Brookes and Cookes of Sheffield. The handles were of solid ivory and on the blade of the knife was engraved: 'On the occasion of the opening of the Denby Dale Great Jubilee Pie, eight feet diameter, two feet deep. 27 August 1887. It was decided that the words 'Presented to Henry J

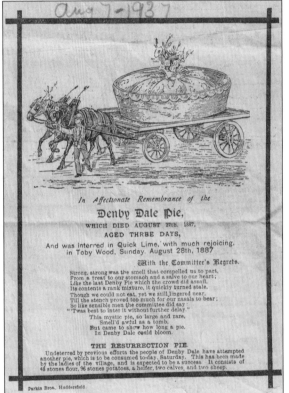

Top-left card:

Strong, strong was the smell that compelled us to part,
From a treat to our stomach and a salve to our heart;
Like the last Denby Pie which the crowd did assail,
Its contents a rank mixture, it quickly turned stale.

Though we could not eat, yet still we lingered near,
Till the stench proved too much for our nasals to bear;
So like sensible men the committee did say:
"'Twas best to inter it without further delay."

This mystic pie, so large and rare,
Smell'd awful as a tomb,
But came to show how long a pie
In Denby Dale could bloom.

Top-right card:

In Affectionate Remembrance of the

Denby Dale Pie,

WHICH DIED AUGUST 27th,

AGED THREE DAYS,

And was interred in Quick Lime, with much rejoicing, in Toby Wood, Sunday, August 28th, 1887.

With the Committee's Regrets.

Middle-left card:

In Affectionate Remembrance of the

Denby Dale Pie,

WHICH DIED AUGUST 27th, 1887,

AGED THREE DAYS,

And was interred in Quick Lime, with much rejoicing, in Toby Wood, Sunday, August 28th, 1887

With the Committee's Regrets.

Strong, strong was the smell that compelled us to part,
From a treat to our stomach and a salve to our heart;
Like the last Denby Pie which the crowd did assail,
Its contents a rank mixture, it quickly turned stale.

Though we could not eat, yet still we lingered near,
Till the stench proved too much for our nasals to bear;
So like sensible men the committee did say:
"'Twas best to inter it without further delay."

This mystic pie, so large and rare,
Smell'd awful as a tomb,
But came to show how long a pie,
In Denby Dale could bloom.

THE RESURRECTION PIE.

Undeterred by previous efforts the people of Denby Dale have attempted another pie, which is to be consumed to-day, Saturday. This has been made by the ladies of the village, and is expected to be a success. It consists of 48 stones flour, 96 stones potatoes, a heifer, two calves, and two sheep.

Parkin Bros., Huddersfield.

Middle-right card:

In Affectionate Remembrance of

THE

DENBY DALE PIE,

WHO DIED AUGUST 27th, 1887,

Aged Three Days,

And was interred in Quicklime, with much rejoicing, in Toby Wood, Sunday, August 28th, 1887.

With the Committee's regrets.

Strong, strong was the smell that compelled us to part,
From a treat to our stomach and a salve to our heart;
But a jubilee pie with so "mongrel" a tale,
Was ne'er a success—hence it quickly turned stale.

We smell thee when the morning dawns,
We smell thee when the night returns,
We smell thee here, we smell thee there,
Thy scent is present everywhere.

Bottom-right card:

In Affectionate Remembrance of the

Denby Dale Pie,

WHICH DIED AUGUST 27th, 1887

AGED THREE DAYS,

And was interred in Quick Lime, with much rejoicing, in Toby Wood, Sunday, August 28th, 1887.

With the Committee's Regrets.

Strong, strong was the smell that compelled us to part,
From a treat to our stomach and a salve to our heart;
But a jubilee pie with so "mongrel" a tale,
Was ne'er a success—hence it quickly turned stale.

Four variations of the Funeral Notice card produced in 1887.

Brierley Esq, should be engraved on top of the blade, but as there was not time for that before the pie was cut, it will have to be done afterwards. The knife and fork obtained in 1846 for Mr James Peace to cut the 'Repeal' pie with are now in the possession of Mr J W Dewhirst of Denby Dale, grandson of Mr James Peace. They were shown in the tent, and it was Mr Dewhirst's intention to have used them on the Jubilee Pie, but we believe he had no opportunity of doing so. Plates with a portrait of the queen in the centre and a suitable inscription on the border, were on sale as mementoes of the occasion.

Sports – It had been arranged that sports should be held whilst the pie was being served and afterwards, but races of any kind were out of the question. Four prizes were given for the best groomed and decorated horses and they were awarded as follows:- 1st 10s Mr John Brierley; 2nd 7s 6d Mr J Mellor; 3rd 5s Mr Lodge; 4th 2s 6d Mr J Brierley. Mr F Fisher, Plumpton House, Thurlstone, and Mr T Milnes, Nether Denby, were the judges. Professor James's Punch and Judy show seemed to attract many; and the 'jubilee jenny slide' a cross between a toboggan and a switchback railway had also many patrons. Denby Dale Brass Band did good service when the gala commenced. The refreshment catering was in the hands of Smart and Townend of Leeds. A display of fireworks by Mr J W Potten of Huddersfield took place in the evening. During the day in addition to the many persons who were crushed and bruised in the struggle about the pie, a Huddersfield man had his leg broken at the slide, and he was carefully removed and tended, under the care of Mr A F Bedford of Barnsley.

NB – The Brierley family originated in Salford and worked as cotton manufacturers. They had arrived in Denby Dale by 1851. John Brierley (the man who cut the pie in the absence of his son, Henry Josiah), lived at Albany House in the village and was recorded as a master dyer employing eleven men. John's death in 1893 aged sixty-one signalled the beginning of the end of the family's sojourn in Denby Dale and by 1912 the name disappears. Henry Josiah was born in 1863 and died in 1909 aged forty-six. He lived at 'Kirkstyles', Cumberworth and played cricket for Cumberworth United during the 1890's.

Chapter 5

3 September 1887

The Resurrection Pie

Pie No. 5

Village pride had taken a serious knock. The 1887 pie had been a disaster, on top of which few of the local people, the old and the very young, had been able to take any part in the day's proceedings. The Committee had underestimated the number of people likely to attend the event, which was by now newsworthy and well known in the North of England. The stories of unplucked and undrawn game birds had been widely reported along with the general stink of the concoction, what could the Committee do to restore their and the village's good name? A major decision had to be made and when it came it was a very brave one indeed. Undeterred by events the previous weekend, the people of Denby Dale made another pie, to be eaten on Saturday 3 September, the weekend following the disaster.

10 September 1887

The Denby Dale Jubilee Celebration – Another Pie.

In our issue last week we reported at length the proceedings attendant on the attempted celebration of the queen's jubilee at Denby Dale.

The pie itself and the whole celebration proved, without any blame to the committee, an undoubted – in fact – a confessed failure, and a veil may well be drawn over it.

The reputation of the village was at stake. It was the traditional place of big pies and its name must be maintained. Failure was not defeat, a second pie should be made, and it should really be a Denby Dale pie, conceived, constructed and carried out to its issue by the people of Denby Dale.

The fifth pie was prepared by the committee of the fourth pie who:

Felt it their duty to provide the inhabitants of the district, who were prevented by the crush from partaking of the previous pie.

This pie was to be made by the ladies of the village and this time there was no publicity, no professional baker and . . . no game. Indeed game was never used again in a Denby Dale Pie. Surprisingly, but as tradition now demanded, a commemorative plate was issued, this time showing two portraits of Queen Victoria, one from the beginning of her reign and the other as she was at the time of the pie.

The *Barnsley Chronicle* continues,

On Saturday last the project was successfully completed, the reputation of the village was maintained, the queen's jubilee was characteristically honoured, and the old people, young children, and inhabitants generally, who had been disappointed, were feasted in the old traditional style. The second pie of the jubilee year came about in this wise. When the remains of the pie of 27 August were disposed of – and over that disposal we will allow that veil to remain – there were still funds in hand; the mighty dish, the serviceable boiler and the well-built oven were still available and ready for use again. On 30 August, three days after the failure, Mr G W Naylor and others met to consider what was to be done. A committee was forenamed consisting of Messrs: G W Naylor, W Lister, Jno McDonald, Geo Barraclough, M Worsley, Jos Blacker, R H Morley and Heap with Mr Wood as secretary.

They obtained the assistance of a committee of ladies viz, Mrs Naylor, Mrs J Wood, Mrs Kaye, Mrs J Hepponstall, Mrs T Hirst, Mrs J Parker, Mrs S Wood, Mrs T Lee, Mrs Revill, Mrs T Wood, Miss Wood, Mrs J Lockwood, Mrs J Hanson, Miss Stephens and Miss F Wood. (These were the ladies who made the pie.)

Other meetings were held, arrangements made and the material for the pie purchased as follows: One beast, 47 stones, one calf, 10 stones, one sheep 89lbs, potatoes 104 stones, flour 48 stones, with lard and other necessaries in proportion. The flour was given out in lots of 2 stones each to the ladies of the village to be made into dough for the pie, and the potatoes were pared or scraped by seven of the men of the village. On Thursday the animals were slaughtered, and on Friday they were cut up, and the making of the pie was commenced. The huge dish, which during the week had been several times washed with hot water and thoroughly cleaned, was again utilised. The meat was stewed under the superintendence of the ladies' committee and, working steadily all day, by soon after 10 o'clock on the Friday night, the pie, which when ready for the oven weighed 320 stones, was completed, and at half past ten o'clock it was placed in the oven, which had been properly heated, to bake. The greatest attention was paid to the cooking of the pie, and at half past three o'clock on the Saturday morning it was decided it was 'enough', it appeared to be cooked to a nicety, and it was taken out of the oven and allowed to cool until the time fixed for the celebration. In the meanwhile it was decorated with bright coloured papers and flowers, and quite a gay appearance was imparted to the huge pie.

The ladies of the village made the pastry in the small hours of Saturday morning, indeed they made two crusts. An inner crust that covered the meat and an outer one that rested on skewers and chicken wire.

The *Barnsley Chronicle* continues,

Afterwards it was drawn to its destination – the scene of the coming feast – at Inkerman Mills, kindly lent for the occasion by Mr Henry Horton Peace. Two horses drew the pie to the mill, and it was accompanied on the route by Inspector Calcraft and a dozen constables. As it reached the mill yard a heavy shower came on, but the pie was hastily covered with canvas and suffered no harm. The experience of an outdoor feast gained the previous week had been quite sufficient to convince the committee that it was not wise to incur any unnecessary risk, beside which, the weather being broken, there was not that promise of, or confidence in, fine weather which there had been the previous week. Inkerman Mills were available, and the pie was taken there. Two large rooms were prepared for the occasion – five tables, each one capable of accommodating sixty guests, were placed in one room for the adults, and three tables

George William Naylor (1845-1888).

of similar dimensions stood in another room for the juveniles. At the time fixed for the feast to commence most of the inhabitants of Denby, Denby Dale and Cumberworth had assembled and the carvers Messrs J H Dewsnap, W Holmes, D Mathews and W Lister – attired in white flannels and duly approned – took their places. Mr G W Naylor then briefly addressed the assembly. He gave to everyone a hearty welcome and said there was abundance of good provision for them, and he hoped that all would enjoy themselves. They had been disappointed on the previous Saturday, he said, and their entertainment had been spoiled by the conduct of a number of people who had behaved like ravenous wild beasts. They would have nothing of that kind that day, he was sure, for they were all their own people.

'We considered that we were under a moral obligation to treat the people in the two townships of Cumberworth and Denby Dale to pie, according to the promise we had made to them.'

He then described how the pie was made and enumerated its contents, and then, amid loud cheers, gave orders for it to be opened. Promptly the carvers obeyed, and the tables in the room being full and the servers in their places the pie was placed into large bowls and carried to the tables. Then plates were quickly filled and the feast began. Each guest was supposed to bring his or her own plate, knife and fork. Some had forgotten to do this and they either borrowed from their friends or ate the pie with their fingers. There was enough and to spare for all. The carvers and servers were kept busy as bees for a couple of hours or so, by the end of which time, the guests, numbering about 2,000, had all been amply supplied. Of course there were some who found fault – that it was too highly seasoned or insufficiently seasoned – that the potatoes were over done or underdone – that it was too rich or not rich enough – that it was underdone or overdone – but reasonable people were generally satisfied, the pie was a complete success, and the guests, as a rule, expressed their approval in the heartiest terms. When the whole of the 2,000 guests had dined off the pie there was still sufficient left to feed another thousand and it was decided that this should be distributed amongst the poor. The feast concluded, sports for the children and others were held in a field near the mills kindly lent for the occasion by Mr Wm. Mellor of Denby, and the 'jenny slide' found many patrons. Owing to the weather the stay in the field was not so long as would otherwise have been the case, and all left in good time, many carrying away with them pieces of the crust of the pie to be kept as mementoes of the second great pie of the jubilee year.

The older residents received a gill of beer and along with the children were given a piece of pie to take home. The committee members had made amends for the previous week's fiasco. The sale of the plates substantially aided the costs of both ventures and when the accounts were drawn up it was found that a profit of £119 14s. 9½d had been made, which was distributed to local charities.

Chapter 6

1 August 1896

The Fiftieth Anniversary of the Repeal of the Corn Laws

Pie No. 6

After an almost hasty gap of only nine years, the Denby Dalers were at it again. Contemporary writers seem to struggle with the reasons for this. Considering the problems that beset the previous two offerings one would have thought the villagers would have wanted to wait a full generation before being subjected to similar events. Undaunted, the fiftieth anniversary of the repeal of the hated Corn Laws was a good enough occasion to warrant such excess again. It is likely that feelings still ran high and that only with the passing of time have we forgotten the deprivation caused by the lack of the availability of bread for the common man. It is also likely that the villagers wished to slay the ghost of 1887 and the embarrassment that went with it. What better way than to bake the most successful pie ever.

The locals had certainly not forgotten their hardships and one man in particular was chosen for the singular honour of leading the procession on the day. Mr Joseph Hirst, by now eighty-eight years old had taken part in the original struggle to have the laws lifted. He had also been present at the 1846 pie. He was to travel in a cart drawn by two grey horses flanked alongside by his two grandsons whose mode of dress represented the expensive loaf whilst the act was in place and the cheap loaf after its repeal. David Bostwick recorded that:

> One in rags and tatters carried a banner bearing the words 'Corn 4 shillings a stone, 1846' and the other one dressed in good West Riding cloth held a placard with the words 'Corn 1 shilling a stone, 1896'.

The pie procession on the Barnsley Road, or K-Line, headed by Joseph Hirst in the cart flanked by his grandsons, Ned Lockwood and Edwin Hirst.

A feature in the *Huddersfield Examiner* dated 7 June 1988 concerned the longevity of a member of my own family, Mr Douglas Heath, the former blacksmith in Denby Dale. He was ninety-five years old when he was interviewed and was only three-and-a-half when the 1896 pie was made, but he still had a mental picture of the parade and remembered being carried up on horseback into the park where the festivities took place. He also remembered the two grandsons of Mr Hirst, he recalled:

> *There were two lads, one with a real smart suit and the other one all in rags. I think they were Ned Lockwood and Edwin Hirst.*

As before a committee was formed, which was detailed on the back of the programme, sold for 1d:

President of the Pie Committee: Frank Naylor. Mr Naylor was the son of George William Naylor (the man responsible for the stone built Denby Dale viaduct), who was instrumental in the creation of the Resurrection Pie of 1887 and whose speech we have noted in the previous chapter.

Pie Servers:
H Gill, T D Mathews, J F Kitson, Sam McDonald, Evan McDonald, W H Lockwood, E Whittaker, John Mellor, H Mellor, Fred Schofield, Sam Jackson, George Exley.

Ticket Sellers:
At the club – Messrs George Dyson, A Haigh, Joe Hirst, Amos Firth, Tom Gaunt, A Gill. In Naylor's Yard – Messrs Joe Hardy, Willie Dalton.

In Kitson's Yard – Messrs H Barrowclough, Luther Hirst.

In Morley's Yard – Messrs Fred Townend, John McDonald.

At the top entrance – Messrs W Castle, James Turton, George Sharp, Tom Castle.

At the band house – Messrs Albert Schofield, James Heppenstall, Harry Whitleley, Arthy Beevers.

Ticket Collectors:

George Perkins, A Lockwood, Joe Haywood, G H Exley, H Morris, Luke Marsden, Willie Thorpe, B Moxon, Fred Haigh, A Acton, Ernest Gaunt, Willie Turton, John Priest, Sam Firth, George Senior, John Firth, Fred Hobson, Joseph Shaw.

Secretary:

C W Haigh.

The lessons of the past had been learned and were duly observed by the committee, who kept faith with local ability in preparing and cooking the pie. Five village experts were to supervise a team of local ladies and the dish used in 1887 was to be scrubbed clean and used again. The experts included:

W Spivey and Fred Dearnley and the women, J Parker, and Mrs Charles Wood of Denby Dale and Mrs Stafford of Ingbirchworth.

The gross weight of the dish with its contents was 35cwts (3,920lbs). The following list of contents now omits all game and poultry:

1,120lbs of beef, 180lbs veal, 112lbs mutton,
60lbs lamb, 1,120lbs flour and 160 lbs lard.

The *Barnsley Chronicle* reported the news of a new pie a week prior to the event on 1 August:

The Monster Denby Dale Pie.

The pie this year is being baked in a dish 10 feet x 6½ feet and 1 feet deep, ³/₈ inch steel plates being used in the manufacture of it and has been specially made by Messrs W C Holmes & Co, Huddersfield, and weighs about half a ton. The knife is 33 inches long and the fork 25 inches long and have been supplied by Mr William Lockwood, jeweller, Victoria Lane, Huddersfield. Mr Fred Horn has kindly granted use of his premises for building the oven and baking the pie and offered the facility for carrying out the objective successfully.

The oven, measuring 9 feet wide, 14 feet long and 2 feet high, was built behind Mr Horn's corn mill in the village by Allot Brothers of Denby Dale. In all the pie weighed 1 ton 15 hundredweight. It took six hours to cook the meat and two-and-a-half hours to bake the crust.

The committee was expecting large crowds to turn up, indeed estimates varied from anywhere between 60,000 and 100,000 people. Again lessons had been learned and the wooden platform in Norman Park, where the pie was to be cut, was solidly built and surrounded with barricading. Further barriers were erected in the field to stop the crowd rushing the platform as the pie was cut. The platform was draped with an awning and bedecked with floral trimmings.

DENBY DALE JUBILEE PIE, 1896.

DENBY DALE PIE

To Commemorate the Repeal of the Corn Laws.

SERVED ON SATURDAY, AUGUST 1ST.

The Pie consisted of 1120 lbs. Beef, 180 lbs. Veal, 112 lbs. Mutton, 60 lbs. Lamb, 1120 lbs. Flour, and 160 lbs. Lard, and was baked in a dish measuring 10ft. long, 6ft. 6in, wide, and 1ft. deep, and the gross weight of dish and contents being about 35 cwts.

The Pie was prepared by a few ladies in the village.

The Pie was conveyed on a Dray drawn by 14 horses, in procession, to Norman Park, where it was cut into by Mr. Frank Naylor.

PREVIOUS PIES.

The first Pie was baked in 1788 (King George III.'s recovery), the second in 1815 (Battle of Waterloo), the third in 1846 (Repeal of the Corn Laws) the fourth in 1887 (Queen's Jubilee), and again in the same year one was baked for the inhabitants who were prevented by the crush from partaking of the previous one.

Details from the 1896 pie programme, available for 1d each on the day.

Denby Dale Jubilee Pie, 1896.

This Pie is in Commemoration of the Repeal of the Corn Laws, 1846.

The oven is designed, and constructed by Messrs. Aliott Bros., of Denby Dale, and its dimensions are 13ft. long 9 feet wide and 2ft. high (inside measurement), and is situated adjacent to Mr. F. Horn's, Corn Mill, by his kind permission.

The dish, which is made of ⅜ inch. steel plates, is 10ft. long, 6ft. 6in. wide and 1ft. deep, has been specially made by Messrs. W. C. Holmes & Co., Huddersfield, and weighs about ½ ton.

The contents of the Pie are as follows :—

Beef 1120 lbs., Veal 180 lbs., Mutton 112 lbs., Lamb 60 lbs., Flour 1120 lbs., and Lard 160 lbs.

The gross weight of dish and contents is about 35 cwts.

The Pie has been prepared by a few ladies in the village, assisted by Messrs. J. W. Spivey, and F. Dearnley, Denby Dale.

The Carvers which are of a very elegant design, with buck horn handles, and silver-mountings, have been supplied by Mr. Wm. Lockwood, Jeweller, &c., Victoria Lane, Huddersfield. The knife is 33 inches long (with suitable inscription on blade), and the fork 25 inches long.

The Proceeds realized from the Celebration, after all expenses have been paid, will be devoted to Local Charities.

Programme for the Day,
AUGUST 1st, 1896.

10 a.m.—The Pie leaves the oven, for Norman Park, drawn by 14 Horses.

11 to 4—The Pie will be on view in the Park

3 p.m.—Procession of Band, Waiters, &c., from the White Hart Inn.

4 p.m.—Presentation of Carvers by Mr. W. Wood to Mr. Frank Naylor, who will then cut into the Pie.

4-30 p.m.—Serving of Pie to the general public.

SELECTIONS OF MUSIC BY THE
Denby Dale Prize Brass Band
DURING THE AFTERNOON.

VARIETY COMPANY,
Under the direction of
Mr. G. BURTON, F.O.S., of Sheffield,
THE CELEBRATED CATERER.

NINE TURNS.

Grand Display of Fireworks
At dusk by J. W. Potter & Sons, Dalton, Huddersfield.
REFRESHMENTS on the GROUND
Refreshment Caterer :—Mr. F. Hoult, Chetham St., Sheffield.

No Pass-out Checks.

The Committee reserve the right to alter the Programme if necessary.

Denby Dale Pie.

This romantic and enterprising village has always been renowned for its Pies. Its history in this respect being without an equal in the annals of the whole world.

The first Pie was baked in 1788, in commemoration of King George III's recovery from his terrible mental affliction, the recovery being marked by universal rejoicing throughout England. The Pie was baked in a field called Cliffe Style Field, just behind the White Hart Inn.

The Second Pie was made in 1815, in honour of the great peace which was ratified after the Battle of Waterloo and defeat and downfall of Napoleon I.

Its contents were half a sheep, 20 fowls, and half a peck of flour.

The Pie was baked in the kiln attached to the Denby Dale Corn Mill.

The Third Pie was in commemoration of the Repeal of the Corn Laws, and was held on August 19th, 1846.

Its contents were 44½ stones flour, 91½lbs. suet, 19lbs. lard, 16lbs. butter, 7 hares, 14 rabbits, 2 brace pheasants, 2 brace partridges, 2 brace grouse, couple ducks, couple geese, pair turkeys, pair guinea fowls, 2 pairs common fowls, 6 pigeons, 63 small birds, 5 sheep, 1 calf, and 100lbs. beef.

This pie was baked in a bakery at Cuck Stool, or the Ducking Stool, Denby Dale. It was successfully baked, and put on to a platform to be cut up and served. However, the platform gave way, and the pie slipped on to the ground. A crowd of 15,000 people surged forward, a scramble ensued, and amid a wild state of turmoil and riot the stage was utterly demolished and the pie flung to the winds.

The Fourth Pie was in honour of the Jubilee of our gracious Queen Victoria, and further to shew the world we are true to the traditions of our forefathers.

The oven was designed and built by Messrs. Jonas Drake & Sons, Halifax and was completed in ten days by five men. It measured 14 feet square outside, and ten feet square within, lined and contrived to equalise the heat in all parts, and situated near the White Hart Inn. The bricks were supplied by Mr. Joe Kitson, Denby Dale. The oven contained 3000 red bricks, 5000 fire bricks, and 500 enamelled faced bricks, and 20 cwt of fire clay.

One boiler adjoining, to stew the meat, was capable of holding 80 gallons, and was supplied by Mr. Joseph Barraclough, Denby.

The dish was made of sheet and angle iron, rivetted together, weighing 15 cwts., and was made by Messrs. W. C. Holmes & Co., Huddersfield.

The size of this pie was 8ft. in diameter, and 2 feet deep, and the baker was Mr. F. Workman, Halifax.

The knife was 30 inches long, and the fork two feet long.

The contents of the Pie was :—Flour 60 stones, beef 850 lbs. mutton 160 lbs., veal 160 lbs., lamb 140 lbs., lean pork 250 lbs., lard 100 lbs., butter 50 lbs., rabbits 32, hares 3, fowls 42, pigeons 48, grouse 12, ducks 6, plovers 4, turkey 1, geese 5, small birds 100.

The whole contents weighed about 200 stones, or 1 ton 5 cwt.

The Fifth Pie was prepared for Sept. 3rd, 1887, by the Committee of the Fourth Pie, who felt it their duty to provide the inhabitants of the District, who were prevented by the crush, from partaking of the previous pie.

A timetable of the events on offer on the day was listed in the programme thus:

10.00am – The pie leaves the oven for Norman Park, drawn by fourteen horses.
11.00am – 4.00pm – The pie will be on view in the park.
3.00pm – Procession of band, waiters, etc. from the White Hart Inn.
4.00pm – Presentation of carvers by Mr W Wood to Mr Frank Naylor who will then cut into
the pie.
4.30pm - Serving of the pie to the general public.

In another new initiative, the local medical officer of health had been placed in charge of confirming that the pie was fit to eat. Doctor Duncan Alistair McGregor was the first person to pass a medical opinion on the quality of the finished product. With an undoubted sigh of relief by the committee, his verdict was that it was good and wholesome and the pie was loaded on to its wagon, covered by a white cloth and decked with flowers.

The pie, out of the oven and draped with a white cloth aboard Fred Horne's wagon, outside the corn mill. Frank Naylor is the man in the centre. *(West Yorkshire Archive Service/Tolson Museum.)*

The pie outside the corn mill with the cooks who baked it.

A very rare though poor copy of the 1896 committee surrounding the pie.

Ready for off, the mounted police escort awaits.

In front of the White Hart amidst the crowds.

A very rare, though poor copy of a photograph of the pie as it travelled along the Barnsley Road, a young bullock takes a great interest in the proceedings.

The procession halts for a photograph underneath one of the viaduct arches.

(West Yorkshire Archive Service/Tolson Museum.)

41

The *Barnsley Chronicle* – 8 August 1896.

The Denby Dale pie, of which we gave the geometrical dimensions with a list of ingredients in our last, was opened on Saturday afternoon in the presence of a large crowd of interested spectators and amid numerous demonstrations of rejoicing. The attendance however was not as numerous as had been anticipated, this circumstance being probably due to the fact that Denby Dale pies had been rather plentiful of late, and that, as a consequence, the gloss of their novelty has been to some extent worn off. The pie was baked in an oven 13 feet long, 9 feet wide and 2 feet high, inside measurement, and was contained in a dish 10 feet long, 6 feet 6 inches wide and 1 foot deep.

In the morning the pie was drawn through the village by fourteen horses and was safely deposited in Norman Park, and at four o'clock it was opened after a small formal ceremony. The Denby Dale Brass Band, which played selections in the park during the afternoon and evening, marched along with a small army of waiters from the White Hart Inn to the park, and shortly after the waiters had taken their respective positions, Mr William Wood presented a pair of carvers with black horn handles and silver mountings to Mr Frank Naylor who then cut into the pie. Before doing so, however, he informed those waiting that he had a letter from the Medical Officer of Health declaring the contents of the pie to be pure, sweet and wholesome. They listened patiently to the carefully chosen phrases in which Mr William Wood sang a panegyric on Denby Dale pies, and hurled back with lofty scorn the insults and jibes thrown at the Dale because of the fiasco attending the jubilee pie of 1887.

Mr Wood:
The peculiarity of Denby Dale is the power to make the finest pie in the whole universe – every true Daler admits that peculiarity and rejoices in it.

Denby Dale, he assured the waiting thousands, was determined to hold its place as the greatest pie makers in the universe. Mr Wood handed to Mr Naylor, the president of the committee, the knife, rivalling a long sword and the fork, to match.

Mr Naylor:
This pie is not such a wonderful mechanical mixture as the 1887 pie, which might, from its contents, have been specially designed for Li Hung Chang. But it is, as Mark Twain has it, a good, competent pie.

Nine years previously, Mr Naylor continued, it had been decreed by circumstances beyond their control that the celebration of that year was not the success they had expected.

Since then, tens of thousands of taunts have been hurled at us, from north, south, east and west, that we could not make a successful pie. We decided to bear the taunts patiently, to use local talent, and to wipe away the stigma most effectively. I ask you ladies and gentlemen to partake with me of this glorious pie.

The president shouldering the weapons flourished them aloft and dashed into the crust. More appropriate would it have seemed if he had attacked it with mattock and shovel, and the people cheered while the waiters stood expectant by, ladles in hand. Underneath the crust was

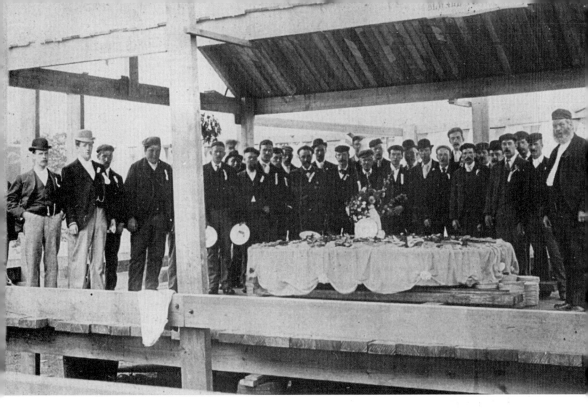

Frank Naylor, second from the left, and the rest of the Pie Committee on the well-built timber stage prior to the opening ceremony. Note the sign informing people to be wary of pickpockets on the canopy roof, top right. *(West Yorkshire Archive Service/Tolson Museum.)*

Frank Naylor finishes his speech and cuts the 1896 pie.

The ceremonial knife and fork used by Frank Naylor in 1896, now on display at Denby Dale Pie Hall.

Detail of the inscription to Frank Naylor on the 1896 ceremonial knife.

a supporting cover of wire netting and this in turn was born up by transverse bars of steel. Then the visitors filed in one by one. Some had secured their plates beforehand. These were picturesquely adorned and suitably inscribed with the date and a statement of the occasion of the celebration. A shilling each was charged for the plates and as the bearers filed in they paid another shilling for a helping of the pie.

The plates provided numbered 2,350 and many were still purchasing hours after the pie was opened. The stream of purchasers was continuous. Knives and forks were not provided. Some tasted the pie as they sat on the sward. Most of the buyers wrapped it up, plate and meat together, in paper, and then fastening it up in a handkerchief bore it away to form a subject for discourse by the hearth. The elaborate precautions were entirely successful. Mounted police and police on foot guarded the enclosure. With a keen diagnosis of the form sometimes taken by despair, the large pond on the lower ground beyond the platform was securely barricaded. No disappointed spectator attempted to burst the barriers and seek a watery 'surcease from sorrow'. On the higher ground another platform was devoted to a variety performance of another kind, under the direction of Mr George Burton of Sheffield, an impresario who caters for outdoor

A Warner Gothard souvenir poster from 1896, showing the pie inside the oven.

galas and demonstrations where rustic revels are in progress. Lady acrobats, wire walkers and male comedians who satirised the militia, held an amused crowd, in the intervals they stole from gazing on the pie and watching its demolition. The pie and the attendant preparations cost £250. If there is a balance of profit the money will be devoted by the Denby Dale Club, who managed the celebration, to local charities.

Around 2,000 portions were issued by the twelve servers. The day's festivities continued during and after the serving, with the Denby Dale Brass Band played throughout the afternoon, the Variety Company supplied nine different acts and a 'Grand Display of Fireworks' rounded off what had turned out to be a very successful day. The organisers could breathe a sigh of relief. They had buried the memories of nine years before.

Chapter 7

28 August 1928

The Huddersfield Infirmary Pie

Pie No. 7

It took the people of Denby Dale a long time to decide to bake another pie, thirty-two years had passed since the success of 1896 and a new generation had never experienced this most singular of village traditions.

Queen Victoria's long reign had ended with her death in 1901 and two further coronations had followed, those of Edward VII and later that of George V in 1910. Neither occasion had led to a Denby Dale pie being baked to celebrate. This was followed by World War One, which saw millions of the nation's young men leave home shores never to return. The carnage of the trenches and the beginning of the development of modern warfare left few with any desire for the levity of such occasions as a Denby Dale pie. Denby Dale did, however, pull its weight during the conflict by converting the village memorial hall into a military hospital from December 1916 to February 1919, admitting 924 patients during that time.

The relief created by the cessation of hostilities was tempered by the austerity it had caused which rendered any possibility of a Denby Dale Pie being made to celebrate the end of the War impractical and any ideas were soon abandoned.

Ten years after the war, Huddersfield Royal Infirmary urgently required funds to improve its services, which was the major factor in the decision to venture forth and bake again. Before the inauguration of the National Health Service, hospitals depended very much on voluntary contributions, indeed almost every church and chapel in the country had an 'Infirmary Sunday', where the collection was used solely for the benefit of the local hospital.

At a public meeting it was decided that a much belated 'Victory Pie' would best show the village's appreciation for the work of the hospital, and to this end work began. One thousand pounds was needed to endow a cot in the hospital, to be known as the 'Denby & Cumberworth Cot'. Many of the older residents regarded this late date as a delayed celebration for the end of the war and anyway, it had been thirty-six years since the last one, at least the local newspapers could not now say that Denby Dale pies had been rather plentiful of late.

The whole village became involved with the preparations, every house was decorated with a view to get the village looking its best for the estimated 60,000 visitors expected, and the local newspapers began to report on the tales emanating from the village. Tickets for the field were being sold in London, Newcastle, Hull, Birmingham and many other major cities and special trains and coaches were being laid on. The public houses in the village requested extended opening hours. Ernest Moorhouse of the Prospect Hotel (now The Dalesman) and J H Lockwood of the Forester's Inn, Lower Cumberworth, requested that they be allowed to open from 10am to 3am and from 5.30pm to 10.30pm. Both requests were granted.

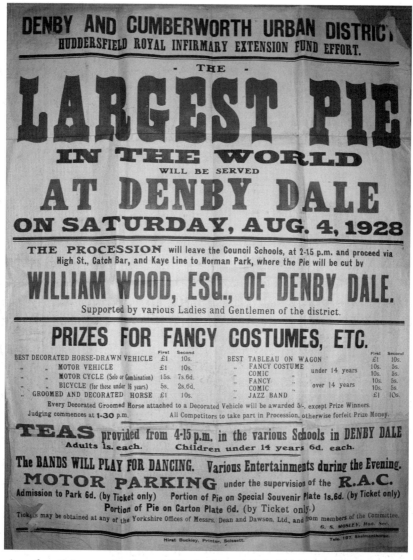

48   An advertising poster from 1928, the lettering is in blue and red.

An expectant village, Wakefield Road, Denby Dale, the day before the pie. The premises of J H Green can be seen to the left. Note the board advertising the pie bolted to the side of the Prospect Hotel.

The banners and bunting are up and the people take a big deep breath before pie day, this view shows the bottom of Miller Hill and the bridge across the River Dearne.

Looking towards Wakefield Road from the bottom of Miller Hill, as the corn mill is prepared for cooking to commence in the background.

Some of the employees of Naylor's Brick and Tile works, sat in the pie dish they had created.

More of the men of Naylor's with the huge dish.

Because this was going to be the biggest pie to date the old dish was now redundant and a new one was built. It measured 16 feet long, 5 feet wide and 15 inches deep, weighing, 1 ton 15cwt, it was made by Mr G W Naylor, of Naylor's Brick and Tile Works, Denby Dale.

A story printed in the 1964 Pie Souvenir Programme commemorates the feeling of one of the employees of Naylor Bros who had evidently worked upon the pie dish:

'Another story I like is of the grandfather of the present oven builder, Mr George Naylor, who like his grandson was possessed of an extremely able and inventive mind. One of the workmen was heard to say "I hope someone keeps the bugger awake tonight, or he'll dream up something else for us to do".

The Denby Dale Concrete Manufacturing Co built an oven at the corn mill on the corner of Wakefield Road and Miller Hill. Ruth Whitwam remembered that the labourers were: Edwin Allot, Joe Noble, Albert Brown, John Hirst, Harry Bedford, Walker Williamson, Arthur Smith, Norman Whiteley, James Ronald Whitwam and Wright Beaumont.

The *Huddersfield Examiner* 1928:

The last brick was placed on the oven on Tuesday night by Mr W H West and the dish was despatched from the works of Messrs Naylor Bros on Wednesday. The dish, of riveted steel plates, weighed 35cwt, which is as much of the weight of the last dish and pie put together. Cranes and levers and jacks had to be brought into service to get it onto the big motor wagon that was to bear it in triumph through the district.

To fill this giant dish the quantity of ingredients had to be suitably increased but, thankfully, not the variety:

4 bullocks, 600lbs of beef, 15 cwt of potatoes, 80 stones of flour, 2 cwt of lard and 2 stones of baking powder.

The oven at the corn mill and the men who built it who included: Edwin Allot, Joe Noble, Albert Brown, John Hirst, Harry Bedford, Walker Williamson, Arthur Smith, Norman Whiteley, James Ronald Whitwam and Wright Beaumont.

Work progresses on building the huge oven.

The pie dish, being taken from its place of manufacture at Naylor Brothers, to the oven at the corn mill.

This meant that there was 100 cubic feet of pie, which was enough for 20,000 people to have nearly ¼lb each.

Responsibility for cooking the pie fell to five local butchers, Mr W A Heap (who was also chairman of the Pie Committee), Mr G T M Lea, Mr Norman Naylor, Mr Tom Schofield and Mr George Senior who were aided by eighteen local women who were chosen as cooks, including: Mrs Crossland, Mrs Firth, Mrs Barrowclough, Mrs Cunningham, Mrs Littlewood, Mrs Stanger, Mrs Mosley, Mrs Lockwood, Mrs Senior, Mrs Wood, Mrs Cooper and Mrs Mosley who were led by Mrs Jonas Kenyon (of Kenyon's Textile Manufacturers on Dearnside).

They were also able to call upon the help of Mr William Wood (secretary of the Pie Committees of the 1887 and 1896 pies).

The meat for the pie was cooked in the ambulance hall, next to the oven whilst the pastry, which had been rolled into small portions, was made in the Salvation Army building across the road. It took a week to cook the meat, in batches, which was then frozen before finally being placed into the pie dish to bake. The dish was constructed into squares to try to ensure that the pastry crust would not sink. Fat cakes were also made so that everyone could have some crust to go with their pie. On the Wednesday night a rehearsal was undertaken and though initially problems occurred whilst trying to remove the dish from the oven due to the confined space, hundreds of people lined the route to be taken and the band played amidst the bunting and decoration – it was carnival time early.

On the night of Thursday 26 August the dish was filled with its pre-cooked delicacies. David Bostwick noted that:

> *A local man, Joseph Kaye, wheeled away six barrow loads of what would have been bad pie that night. Nothing was said to the Public Health Inspector. Nor was he told that the pie dish leaked, and that to stop the gravy trickling away a poultice made of oatmeal and other things was stuffed into the dish to plug the gap.*

Five fine bullocks, grazing quietly at Rockwood Hall, ignorant of their doom, they were to be slaughtered for the Denby Dale Pie.

The women who made the 1928 pie. Standing left to right: J Hinchliffe, T Barraclough, W Lockwood, G H Schofield, Unknown, R Barber, A Atkin, ? Rowlings, J Mosley. Seated left to right: J Crossland, Unknown, T Gelder, Unknown, J Kenyon, F Stanger, J Wood, W Dronfield, W Cunningham.

The ladies and girls making the crust for the pie in the Salvation Army Hall.

The ladies of Denby Dale making the pastry mixture for the pie.

The meat was cooked in boilers before being placed in the huge dish.

Lady Narah Hinchliffe, the wife of Sir James Peace Hinchliffe, chairman of the West Riding County Council, and her daughter, Mabel, seen visiting the oven where the giant pie was to be baked.

The monstrous dish was mounted on wheels to enable the cooks to wheel it in and out of the fire to observe the baking process. The thirty hours baking ticked away, there was little sleep and the pie itself was guarded to prevent the unforeseen. The *Huddersfield Examiner* noted that, 'Odorous whiffs were borne on a light breeze throughout the village.'

All A-Bustle at Denby Dale

Getting the Great Pie Ready for its Night in the Oven

The work on the world's biggest meat and tatie pie reached today the point when all who have anything at all to do with its construction were in such a hurry that they had not the time to stop a second to exchange a word with anyone.

A man tore up one of the village's back streets today with a bar of iron in each hand. He dashed into a blacksmith's shop and flung one bar of iron on the anvil. In less time than it takes to tell he had drawn a sketch of the shape to which he wanted the iron bending, then, without wasting a word, he hurried on to the second blacksmith's shop, where he drew another sketch and deposited the second bar of iron. Then he tore back to the building which has been turned into the oven for the pie and there superintended the cutting of a hole in the top of the oven, through which the bakers will be able to keep an eye on the pie tonight.

It was the same in the long hut where the meat was boiled in a battery of gas coppers. Here on a dozen tables was the flesh of five prime bullocks and the additional 600lbs of beef required for the pie dish, which has a capacity of 100 cubic feet.

The butchers of the village stayed up all last night to cut the meat, and today an army of women finished the job and saw to its preliminary preparation in the boilers. Women in the basement of the Salvation Army Hall were preparing 80 stones of flour, 2 stones of baking powder and 200 weights of lard for the pie crust.

Work on the filling of the pie dish was started at noon and the actual baking process will begin this evening. The fire has been lit and the oven is complete. There is a winch outside by means of which the pie dish will be drawn along a track into the oven.

Finally, at 1pm on Saturday the 28th, the pie was adjudged to be 'well done' and then the first official problem occurred, it was stuck in the oven. The wagon was waiting, the procession was due to begin at 2.15pm, what to do? 'T' pie's bigger than thou thawt,' called a witty, but concerned observer.

The *Sheffield Daily Telegraph:*

The Denby Dale Pie – How It Refused to Leave the Oven – 20,000 Hungry Guests

A large importation of mounted and foot police was unceasingly on alert to keep avenues clear. As the time passed and the fragrance was emitted in little clouds of vapour from the oven, excitement became more intense and the press of people in the immediate vicinity of the oven continued to grow.

To a burst of cheering the huge dish was seen to be moving smoothly from its darkened recess. Then the unforeseen happened. The pie stopped dead, and try as they would the helpers could not budge it. There followed an hour of tense and nerve wracking suspense. The pie, half in and half out of the oven, was an object of pity instead of gladness. It appeared that sufficient iron rollers had not been placed in position and the enormous weight of the pie and its dish – something like 5 tons – had scorned one of its timber supports and crushed it. All kinds of expedients were tried without avail or at most by the gaining of an extra inch. Men with perspiration pouring down their faces wrestled with iron bars. Jacks, roller and iron girders were brought into play and at one time there were over a score of panting helpers struggling to free the Denby Dale pie.

'T pie's bigger then thou thawt' observed a worthy Yorkshire visitor. The bustle continued for over an hour and then by strategy and sheer strength the attackers were rewarded by getting a real move on the part of the pie. A couple of feet remained to be negotiated and this was done by jacking the dish up and backing the lorry the distance between.

Some of the ladies who baked the pie pose for a photograph with the decorated pie wagon, prior to the pie being removed from the oven. *(Susan Buckley collection.)*

£1000 NEEDED FOR HUDDERSFIELD INFIRMARY.
The Largest Pie in the world!
THE PELICAN ENGINEERING COMPANY LTD   T.B.&H.FIRTH   AEC
DENBY DALE

DENBY DALE PIE, AUG. 4TH 1928

The pie gets stuck in the oven.

Crowbars, jacks and manpower finally see the pie out of the oven and on to the back of the lorry.

Large crowds gathered to watch 'the crisis', Miller Hill can be seen in the background.

The oven after the pie's removal, showing some of the apparatus used to winch the enormous dish in and out.

The dish is almost loaded onto the wagon as the large crowds await the procession to begin at 3:30pm.

The village children surround the now empty oven and survey the scene of near disaster.

A winch and hawser had done the early work but it later became expedient for men armed with crowbars to begin to try and lever the steaming hot dish away from the oven. These proved insufficient and so were replaced by 10-foot tram rails. Aided by jacks and using short lifts the pie was at last persuaded away from its tomb, even then only after knocking part of a wall down. One local man, when asked by a reporter what was wrong, replied 'too many bosses'. Only for another problem to surface. The wagon was made of soft wood. By the time the pie was only half way on, it was sinking into the platform. Willing volunteers were then required to place steel rails underneath before the job was done. It was now 3.15pm. The delay in removing the pie from the oven had thrown the day's timetable completely out of gear. Two hundred and fifty helpers in all kinds of costumes armed with large spoons awaited the rush.

The women who baked the pie are aboard their vehicle and wait to join the procession.
(West Yorkshire Archive Service/Tolson Museum.)

The pie begins its journey around the village.

The half-mile-long procession begins to assemble amidst the crowds.

The procession is underway.

Large crowds almost impede the path of the pie vehicle on Wakefield Road.

Every vantage point is used as the procession continues on Wakefield Road.

The pie passing the White Hart.

A Zulu warrior leads the Denby Dale Brass Band in the procession.

An expectant crowd are kept entertained by the procession.

The procession on Wakefield Road. The Sunbeam limousine behind the pie vehicle belonged to John Hinchliffe (1859-1935), son of Zaccheus. It was being driven by his then chauffeur, George Senior of Hartcliffe View.

The women who baked the Pie reach the chemist shop on Wakefield Road.

The old pie dish of 1887/1896 took its place in the days proceedings.

The crowds gather round to inspect the various floats involved in the parade. *(Susan Buckley collection.)*

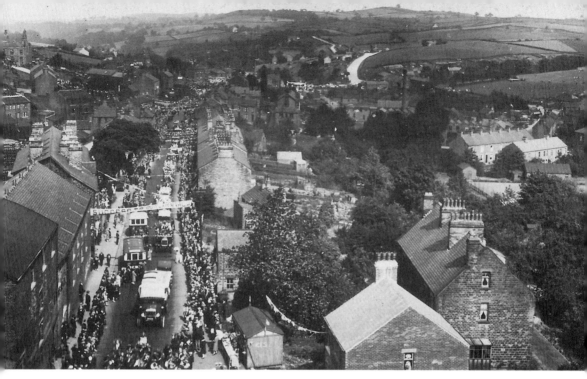

The pie parade in full swing, taken from the top of the viaduct. To the left are Kitson's pipe works. To the right, the field immediately above the houses is Norman Park. A few people can be seen and one marquee, right at the edge of the photograph.

Denby Dale Band, leading the pie under the viaduct and out of the village towards Cumberworth.

The huge procession has by now turned at Catch Bar and moved onto the Kaye Line (Barnsley Road).

The pie is still supported by large crowds as it begins to near its final destination.

A closer view of some of the vehicles taking part in the parade.

The horses were led by their owners who kept a close eye on the wagons, to make sure all went smoothly.

Mounted police keep order and clear the way as the pie passes the mill of Z Hinchliffe & Sons.

The pie heading past Dearne View.

The *Huddersfield Examiner* records:

> *It was 3.30pm before the pie was got into position, and a mighty shout arose from the crowd gathered around the oven, which was quickly echoed by the crowds lining the route.*

The half-mile long procession consisted of mounted police, Denby Dale Silver Prize Band, the pie, bakers, cooks, floats, other decorated vehicles and people in fancy dress or representing groups. It passed through the village by way of Catch Bar to Upper Cumberworth and back to Denby Dale via Kaye Line to its destination in Norman Park to massive cheering from the patient and anxiously waiting public. Forty or fifty police were on duty to keep order, but despite the delay great good humour had prevailed. Just before reaching Norman Park as the band was playing *Ilkla' Moor Baht 'At* there was another little mishap. The decorated superstructure of the wagon carrying the pie got caught in the foliage of the overhanging trees and was badly crumpled, giving it a slightly shoddy appearance on arrival in the park.

On to the lorry stepped Mr John Hinchliffe, the chairman of the Urban District Council:

> *This is a red-letter day in the history of this district. We have delivered the goods in fine condition.*
>
> *'Not before time awther!' was the bawled comment from a vociferous and apparently voracious member of the crowd – a crowd numbering at least 40,000.*

Mr Hinchliffe continued:

> *In spite of the criticism addressed to us, I can assure you that we have got sound stuff behind me (meaning the pie). I have never in my time seen such enthusiasm and endeavour shown for an object, this is a unique occasion. You will never see another pie like this one.*

Mr William Wood had been appointed to the task of cutting the pie, a job he was well suited for due to his associations with previous pies. He was the secretary for the Pie Committees of 1887 and 1896 and, as we have seen, also spoke to the crowds in 1896. He married Lucy Brownhill and had two children, Isabel (who married Jonas Kenyon) and Constance. His sister, Florence Ethel Wood, married George Wilfred Naylor, therefore he was very well connected to the industrial leaders in the Denby Dale community. William, born in Denby Dale in 1860, was the grandson of cloth dealer Jonathan Wood and his wife Emma. He spent his childhood living at the family home, Viaduct House on Kaye Line (Barnsley Road). By the age of twenty-one he was a certified elementary teacher and by 1891 was recorded as a schoolmaster. After his marriage in 1892 he took up a teaching position in Greetland where his two daughters were born, but was back in the village by 1911 at Broad Royd, by which time he was working as a provisional clerk. He was also noted to be the local truancy inspector.

Mr Wood used a knife of about a yard long and the fork used at the 1896 ceremony. It had not been possible to make a fork in time for Saturday, though it was subsequently planned to make a matching one with a suitable inscription to Mr Wood. In his speech he spoke of the pride inherent in Denby Dale at its reputation for making monster pies:

The ceremonial carvers are proudly displayed for photographers prior to William Wood making the first cut. The pie is covered by a cloth.

William Wood about to open the 1928 Denby Dale pie.

Knife and fork now sunk deep into the pie, Mr Wood poses for photographs. Crouching on the opposite side is Edward Hobson. Behind him in the chefs hat is Thomas Heap. The man next to Mr Heap leaning on the wagon is Joseph Kay.

The formalities now almost complete, William Wood poses for a final picture. *(West Yorkshire Archives/Tolson Museum.)*

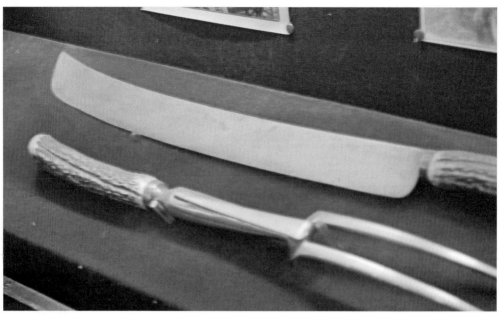

The ceremonial knife and fork, now on display at Denby Dale Pie Hall.

Expectant crowds try to get the best view in Norman Park in order to see William Wood cut the pie.

When we in Denby Dale received the invitation to join in the common effort to help the Huddersfield Royal Infirmary it was debated as to what form the effort should take. Should we imitate other villages and have a little tin-pot carnival or a garden party and send up the enormous sum of £20 or £30? This idea fell flat and the effort nearly died at its birth – but rescue was forthcoming. A modest heroine whispered 'Why not have a pie?' This touched the real Denby Dale spirit. The effort sprang at once from a grasping infant into a mighty giant with a driving force that no power on earth could withstand. Unanimously and enthusiastically all sections joined together – the religious bodies, the trades-people, the women and the householders – to make the effort a success.

'Ger into that pie!'

The famished interrupter chimed in again, at which the crowd broke into laughter. The hint was taken:

Mr Wood then took from their case the giant pair of carvers and, wielding them aloft for all to see, stabbed the great pie to the accompaniment of a roar of cheers. The crust of the pie had sagged in parts, but generally it looked appetising enough.

Alongside stood a small army of first comers and when the pie was opened, they, with enormous ladles, proceeded to fill nine zinc baths with the steaming and good smelling product. The baths were passed on to the long rows of serving tables and in a very few seconds the attack of the 20,000 hungry souls who had waited so long for their precious pie had commenced in real earnest.

An army of 256 servers was needed to distribute the pie:

Sixteen to ladle from large bowls to soup plates.
Thirty-two to carry bowls and dishes to lorries.
Twenty-four to carry full bowls from lorries to pie tables.
Forty to apportion pie crust on plates.
Sixteen to carry crust plates to pie tables.
Sixty to apportion and distribute the pie.
Twenty to carry full plates to pie tables.
Twelve boys to carry empty plates.
Thirty-six to deal with tickets.

Brawny butchers dug into the pie with long-handled ladles once the crust was removed. They transferred the food into baths, which were in turn emptied into smaller containers. These were then carried to the tables to be put onto the souvenir pie plates and eaten, everyone getting either a piece of crust or a fat cake to go with it, all for a shilling a head. Long queues kept the servers very busy, but finally the dish was emptied and taken back to the oven where, for a small fee, people were allowed to wind it in and out of the oven demonstrating the simplicity of the mechanism.

Prizes were awarded in various categories for: best decorated wagon, motor wagon, motor cycle and suchlike. Indeed my own Great Uncle, Joe Willie Heath, entered into the spirit of the

Some of the ladies who baked the pie pose for a photograph with their creation before serving begins. *(Susan Buckley collection.)*

A piece of crust is displayed as serving begins.

The moment has finally come as anticipation increases amongst the crowd. The wagons of W Barraclough, Joe Kitson & W C Holmes can be seen.

Huge crowds gather around the trestle tables waiting for a piece of pie.

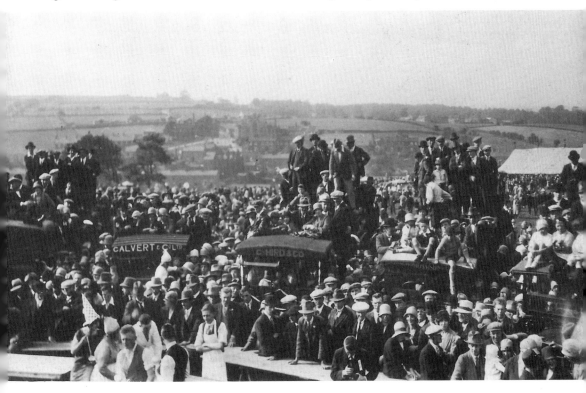

The immaculately dressed servers are kept busy.

Fancy dress was optional but prizes were available for those who took part.

Opinions are formed as the first portions of the pie are devoured.

Good humour amongst the servers kept morale up as they worked to feed the multitude.

The famous Denby Dale Pie Plate is shown to the cameras as more meat and potato is transferred from basin to plate.

Serving the pie continues.

The crowds in Norman Park are gradually served with their pie.

There is no let-up for the servers as pie and crust keep being replenished at the tables for the waiting queues to eat.

Arthur and Hilda Heath find a quieter area of Norman Park to eat their pie.

As cameras were still a novelty, many people went out of their way to be photographed on this special occasion, not least, these servers.

Amidst the crowds, one man feeds himself and his child and finds that the pie is very much to their taste. *(Susan Buckley collection.)*

Satisfied customers relax in the field and take time to examine their pie plates. *(Susan Buckley collection.)*

Laura Heponstall, Lena Heath and Hilda Heath eat their portions of pie whilst Arthur Heath displays the commemorative plate.

Three happy customers amongst thousands. *(Susan Buckley collection.)*

DENBY DALE PIE. AUG. 4TH 1928.   8.

The servers, still busy, under the imposing shadows of Inkerman Mill, across the road from Norman Park. *(Susan Buckley collection.)*

The best bird's eye view available, taken from the top of the pie lorry, looking down upon the proceedings.

A busy, fun-filled day draws towards its end but there is still enough of the enormous pie for the hungry.

occasion when he converted his Morgan three-wheeler motor car into a dummy aeroplane, although he did have to drive to Denby Dale from Upper Denby using the whole width of the road. Some of the winners were:

Best decorated wagon drawn by horses: 1 – A Fowler (Penistone), 2 – E Stafford (Ingbirchworth).
Best decorated motor wagon: 1 – Acton Stoneware Co (Cawthorne), 2 – Scissett Co-operative Society (Olive Green Soap).
Best decorated motorcycle: A Heath (Denby).
Best decorated cycle (under 16): 1 – C Hanson (Denby Dale), 2 – W Firth (Upper Cumberworth).
Best groomed horse: 1 – J Lodge (Denby), 2 – W Butterfield (Lower Denby).
Best tableaux: 1 – Miss Holt and party (Faith, Hope and Charity), 2 – E Biltcliffe (yachting party).
Best fancy costume (under 14): 1 – James Smith (Flour Bag), 2 – Roy Hartley (Chip off the Old Block).
Best comic costume (under 14): 1 – W Seckel (Oranges and Lemons), 2 – C Parker (Pirate).

The day had been, eventually, a great success. It was estimated that between twelve and three o'clock on Saturday between 6,000 and 7,000 people had arrived at Denby Dale station, the bookings from Huddersfield alone totalled 4,016. The financial statement makes for interesting reading and shows that the grand sum of £1147 3s.5d. had been raised for distribution from the

Denby Dale and District Pie and Carnival Effort, 4th August 1928.

FINANCIAL STATEMENT.

INCOME.		£ s. d.	£ s. d.
To Private Subscriptions ...	...	141 18 0	
„ Street and House Collections	...	305 16 2	
„ Street Organ Collections...	...	12 3 5	
			459 17 7
„ Plates and Tickets ...	...	1303 16 7	
„ Utensils and Goods Sold...	...	56 11 9	
„ Refreshments by Ladies ...	...	121 15 3	
„ Rock Sold	...	29 14 0	
			1511 17 7
„ Poetry and Songs	...	...	19 5 9
„ Parking of Cars and Stall Charges ...	...	...	56 6 4
„ Naylors Fund for Sundries	...	...	3 19 0
„ Sundries (General) ...	...	...	5 0 11
„ Bank Interest ...	...	...	1 16 0
			£2058 3 2

EXPENDITURE.		£ s. d.	£ s. d.
By Gross Cost of Oven and Dish	...		113 15 2
„ Contents of Pie ...	...	151 17 3	
„ Less Subscribed by Butchers	...	30 0 0	
			121 17 3
„ Plates Purchased ...	...		387 19 0
„ Rock	...		18 12 3
„ School Rent and Park Field Insurance...	...		10 2 0
„ Utensils	...		97 3 11
„ Procession and Decorations	...		15 14 8
„ Park Field and Entertainments	...		59 19 0
„ Printing, Stationery, Postages, etc.	...		82 2 6
„ Bank Charges (Cheques drawn)	...		9 0
„ Infirmary Bed (Endowment Plate)	...		3 5 0
			£910 19 9

Net Balance for Distribution £1147-3-5
as follows—

	£ s. d.
Huddersfield Royal Infirmary	...1050 0 0
do. do. do.	... 12 3 5
Denby Dale Church of England	... 6 0 0
„ „ Wesleyan Church	... 6 0 0
„ „ Primitive Church	... 6 0 0
„ „ Wes. Reform Church	... 6 0 0
„ „ Salvation Army	... 6 0 0
District St. John Ambulance	... 6 0 0
„ Nursing Association	... 6 0 0
Denby Dale Band ...	... 5 10 0
„ „ Bowling Club	... 5 10 0
„ „ Cricket Club	... 5 10 0
District British Legion ...	... 5 10 0
Cumberworth Church of England	... 3 0 0
„ Reform Church	... 3 0 0
„ Primitive Church	... 3 0 0
„ Cricket Club	... 3 0 0
Denby Church of England	... 3 0 0
„ Band	... 3 0 0
„ Cricket Club ...	... 3 0 0
	1147 3 5
	£2058 3 2

Approved and adopted at a General Meeting of the inhabitants of Denby Dale and District, held at the Denby Dale Church Hut, st July, 1929.

Councillor FRED ELLIS, Chairman,
GRANVILLE S. MOSLEY, General Secretary.

Audited and found correct,
J. E. DALE & Co,
Accountants, BANK CHAMBERS,
WESTGATE, HUDDERSFIELD,

11th day of June, 1929.

Hirst Buckley, Printer, Scissett

The final balance sheet from the 1928 Denby Dale Pie and Carnival effort.

day's proceedings. Huddersfield Royal Infirmary got their cot, situated in the Green Lea Nursing Home, which was an annexe to the hospital, and many other local institutions benefited.

Not quite all the revenue taken managed to make its way to good causes but this far removed from the event we can but smile at the audacity of one local rogue, reported in the local press:

The Tale of Joss Bedford 1928

Joss was the local character who noticed during the 1928 pie that the entrance fee to the Pie Field was 1s 6d. With an ingenuity only surpassed by Robin Hood, Joss betook himself to a secluded part of the other end of the field and, having created a hole in the wall where none existed before, proceeded to admit the pleasantly surprised public at a third of the official price. It was some time before his nefarious activities were spotted, but finally, realising discovery was imminent, he pocketed his ill-gotten gains, fled to the railway station and asked for a ticket. The surprised booking clerk asked 'Where to?', but Joss, with the authorities breathing down his collar, had no time for such details: 'ANY (so-and-so) WHERE!', he gasped, and a train being due, was whisked off to parts unknown.

Long after the pie festivities were over, Joss returned to his native heath to discover forbearance if not forgiveness. After all, reasoned Authority, if we pursue the matter further, the whole story might leak out to the world and our public images might suffer. But one question still remained, just how much had Joss milked from the kitty? The question was eventually put to Joss himself in the local public house, after he had consumed a suitably tongue-loosening pint or two at Authority's expense.

'Na then Joss' said Authority, 'just between thee an me, hah much did ta mak?'

Joss looked around furtively. 'Can ta keep a secret?' he asked.

'Aye, ah can lad', said Authority all ears. Joss drank the remains of his ale.

'Soah can ah!' he said, and left them still wondering.

Unfortunately, the 1928 pie dish had a rather ignoble end as no better use for it could be found other than submerging it in a field behind the railway viaduct and using it as a dew pond.

90

Chapter 8

21 September 1940

The End of the 1887 and 1896 Pie Dish

'Pie Dish for Guns not Butter'

'Pie Dish for Guns, Not Butter' was the cry of the poster announcing the imminent demise of this village relic. The dish had featured in the 1928 pie parade but since that time had found no useful home. Attempts were made by a Mrs Whitwell of Kirkburton and by a Mr T Sheppard of the Hull Municipal Museum to buy the dish. Perhaps Mr Sheppard would have been successful had his timing not clashed with the desire of the villagers to part with it to raise money for the war effort and provide scrap iron. The pie dish was hardly a national treasure and was therefore not immune to the requirements of the time. Mr Douglas Heath remembered that he and his father, Walter, had used the dish for a time, as a 'slaking' trough, at their blacksmith's premises on Wakefield Road. But whether the dish was removed from here to be auctioned or had found another home is unknown. It is likely that they possessed the dish sometime between 1896 and 1928.

The year was 1940, British forces had been evacuated from Dunkirk in June, the Luftwaffe were abroad in the night skies and the Home Guard had been formed, the outlook was bleak. On Saturday 21 September, during the 'Battle of Britain', the Denby Dalers did their bit for the war effort.

A large poster was printed announcing the *Farewell to the 1887 Pie Dish*. Under an escort of the local Civil Defence Services the dish was to be taken to the Central Salvage Dump, its journey would take it through Lower & Upper Cumberworth, Birdsedge, High Flatts and Denby with collections being made along the way. As the poster stated:

BE MORE THAN GENEROUS – our local boys serving in the forces deserve our support.

PIE DISH FOR GUNS—NOT BUTTER

FAREWELL TO THE 1887 PIE DISH

SATURDAY, Sept. 21st, 1940

A PROCESSION of all the Civil Defence Services will escort our HISTORIC PIE DISH to the Central Salvage Dump.

12 noon—The DISH will Start its LAST JOURNEY, via.:—

LOWER CUMBERWORTH, UPPER CUMBERWORTH, BIRDSEDGE, HIGH FLATTS, DENBY.

COLLECTIONS ALL THE WAY

1-45 p.m.—Assembly of Main Procession at Gilthwaites Lane, headed by the Denby Dale SILVER PRIZE BAND.

2-0 p.m.—Move off along WAKEFIELD ROAD to the VIADUCT, returning by HIGH STREET, NORMAN ROAD, and HILLSIDE, to

THE SLADE

3-0 p.m.—**G. H. WILBY,** Esq., will offer the DISH in a series of

AUCTIONS. CERTIFICATES of temporary ownership will be given.

3-30 p.m.—The DISH will be finally handed over to the Chairman of the Council by **FRANK NAYLOR, Esq.**

OTHER ATTRACTIONS:

EXHIBITION of Historic Relics of many Famous Pies, in the COUNCIL SCHOOL, from 10-0 a.m. to 6-0 p.m.   Admission 6d.

COMPETITION—Guess the Weight of the Pie Dish.   Tickets 3d.

Grand Cricket Match

Mr. T. THACKRA'S ELEVEN v. Mr. H. LOCKWOOD'S ELEVEN

Commencing 3-0 p.m.   Admission 6d.

BOWLING—and other events on the Bowling Green.

DEMONSTRATION OF FIRE BOMB CONTROL by Members of the A.F.S., in the SLADE, at 3-45 p.m.

TEA in the MEMORIAL HALL, from 4-15 p.m.   Price 1/-, Children 9d.

SEPT. 20th: A DANCE in the CHURCH HALL, Denby Dale, at 7-30 p.m.   Admission 1/-.

SEPT. 21st: A WHIST DRIVE in the AMBULANCE HALL, Denby Dale, at 7-0 p.m.   Admission 1/-.

SEPT. 21st: A WHIST DRIVE & DANCE in the CHURCH SCHOOL, Cumberworth, at 7 p.m.   1/-

SEPT. 28th: A WHIST DRIVE & DANCE in the CHURCH SCHOOL, Denby, at 7 p.m.   1/-.

BE MORE THAN GENEROUS——OUR LOCAL BOYS

SERVING IN THE FORCES DESERVE OUR SUPPORT, ALL PROCEEDS FROM THESE EVENTS WILL BE USED FOR THEIR BENEFIT.

The PIE DISH will be On View in NORMAN CROFT, from TUESDAY, Sept. 17th.

HIRST BUCKLEY & CO., PRINTERS.

Poster produced to advertise the attractions pertaining to the end of the 1887/1896 pie dish.

A last chance for people to get their photograph taken with the old pie dish in the Slade where it was on display.

The procession was accompanied by the Denby Dale Silver Prize Band. Fundraising events included a 'Grand Cricket Match' between Mr Thackra and Mr Lockwood's elevens, where admission was 6d. A competition to guess-the-weight-of-the-pie-dish, and an exhibition of pie relics in the council school organised by headmaster, Sam Shepley. Bowling and whist drives and dances were held in Denby Dale, Denby and Birdsedge.

At 3.00pm in the Slade, Mr G H Wilby offered the dish in a series of auctions where temporary certificates of ownership were given; this alone raised the sum (according to the balance sheet) of £89 10s. 0d. – the owners not keen to keep such a monstrous thing in their front rooms. A few rusted pieces of the dish were broken off and sold independently, but eventually the bulk of it handed over to the chairman of the council by Mr Frank Naylor. An appropriate choice, as we have already noted, as it was Frank Naylor who made the ceremonial first cut into the 1896 pie.

The dish had been on view in Norman Croft since Tuesday 17 September but was now on its final journey, never to be seen again in Denby Dale.

DENBY DALE 1887 PIE DISH FUND.   21st September 1940.

Balance Sheet

TO:	£.	s.	d.	BY:	£.	s.	d.
STREET COLLECTIONS:				ADVERTISEMENT:			
Denby Dale & Denby £11-5-5				Huddersfield			
(per Mr.Haydn Senior)				Examiner -		8.	0.
Lower Cumberworth £1-10-6							
(per Mr.Frank Mosley)							
Birdsedge & High Flatts				Printing,			
£1-4-1				Ledgers and			
(per Mr.Ben Mitchell)	14.	0.	0.	Postages -	4.	2.	6.
Exhibition of Pie Relics -	7.	0.	1.				
(per Mr. Shepley)				BALANCE:			
Cricket Match -		19.	4.	Cash in Hand			
(per Mr. P. Brown)				6. 6. 7.			
Bowling Club -		15.	0.	Cash at Bank			
(per Mr. Clarkson)				163.16. 7.	170.	3.	2.
Guessing Competition -	8.	5.	1.				
(Weight of Pie dish)							
Profit on Tea -	2.	9.	2.				
SOCIAL EFFORTS:							
Whist Drive (Ambulance Hall)	4.	3.	0.				
(per Mr. C. Beevers)							
DANCE (Church Hall)	8.	12.	0.				
(per Mrs. MacFarlane)							
Whist Drive & Dance -							
Cumberworth.	12.	0.	0.				
(per Mr.Mosley & Mr.Hollingworth)							
Whist Drive & Dance (Denby)	11.	11.	0.				
(per Miss Shaw)							
The White Hart Hotel -	4.	4.	0.				
(per Mr. Hollingworth)							
The Prospect Hotel -	3.	0.	0.				
(per Mr. Kaye)							
Birdsedge - (per Mrs.Allott)	2.	0.	0.				
SUBSCRIPTIONS:	6.	5.	0.				
AUCTION of PIE DISH:	89.	10.	0.				
(88 Certificates issued)							
	£174.	13.	8.		£174.	13.	8

Accounts audited and found correct,
        ARTHUR GILL.   ISABEL KENYON.
                 25. 10. 40.   Treasurer.

In presenting this final Balance sheet
the Committee want to take the opportunity of
conveying their warmest thanks to everyone who has
helped in any way to achieve this wonderful result.

Balance sheet from the 1940 auction of the dish detailing a healthy profit.

Chapter 9

5 September 1964

To Celebrate Four Royal Births
The Village Hall Pie

Pie No. 8

It might be thought odd that the village did not celebrate the end of World War Two and the defeat of Nazi Germany in its usual tradition, but as with the situation after the end of World War One, food restrictions and rationing rendered any such thoughts impractical. The coronation of Queen Elizabeth II in 1953 would also have been another excellent opportunity to bake again, but food restrictions were still in place. Although the desire was there the application for the necessary meat and fat for such a monster pie was naturally turned down, even though £203 had already been raised in the village in anticipation. An attempt was made from an unlikely source to enable the event to go ahead. The Farmers and Settlers Association, of New South Wales in Australia offered Denby Dale 1,400lbs of beef, the idea being that the British government would release the meat from their stocks and that the Australians would replace it. Unfortunately time was against the opportunity and the arrangements could not be made before the coronation and so the offer was turned down.

From 1964 pie brochure:

The 1964 pie story begins with a lady named Nora Kitson, the widow of one of Denby Dale's oldest families. She started it, or the lecturer, whose stories of ancient pies inspired Mrs Kitson to write to the press, castigating Denby Dalers for their lack of enterprise in allowing the tradition of the pie to lapse.

Her activities inspired a meeting, which took place at the Victoria Memorial Hall, to debate and decide the issue.

Mrs Kitson had been promised ingredients, a dish, dray and full coverage from ITV. At the meeting in 1963 the decision was taken to embark on work culminating in the biggest Denby Dale pie ever. An initial fund raising target of £5,000 was set and it was decided to cater for 100,000 people. With a new generation of people to impress and after a thirty-six-year gap preparations began. The members of the meeting voted unanimously for the pie, with a view to building a new community hall as its purpose. Any extra profit was to benefit the National Playing Fields Association, but many people thought that the pie should also be baked to commemorate a national event. The committee, comprising of John Hinchliffe (chairman), William Kenyon, John Netherwood (publicity), Hector Buckley, Monica Turton, Norah Kitson Smith, Jane Beevers, George Naylor, Peter Lenton, Brian Kitson and Alan Cooper struggled with this. They were then presented with the perfect answer, four rroyal babies were expected in the same year for the first time in 200 years. The four were Prince Edward, Lady Helen Windsor, Lady Sarah Armstrong Jones and James Ogilvy. How obliging of the Royal family.

Some of the members of the 1964 Pie Committee, chairman, John Hinchliffe is seated in the centre in the light jacket.

Though there is not enough space within these pages to comment upon all the people involved with the 1964 pie, the following were prominent, though they were not alone. John Hinchliffe was a director of Denby Dale firm Z Hinchliffe & Sons Ltd. His father was involved in the 1928 celebrations, though John was described as 'up to his neck' in 1964. John Netherwood was a director of a Huddersfield printing company and had a special interest in the pie as his father was one of those responsible for trying to revive the Denby Dale tradition back in 1952. Hector Buckley was at the time a farmer of 100 acres at Dry Hill, with another 275 acres around the district. He played a leading role in making arrangements with fellow landowners for the loan of 400 acres of pasture to be lent for the day and gave the use of his new milking parlour for the baking of the pie.

The committee took every possible step to ensure success. Veterans of the 1928 pie were consulted and gladly gave advice though none wished to take an active part, the rule was set - one man – one pie, although two men proved an exception to the rule. Joseph Kaye and Edward Hudson were cooks in 1928 and agreed to help bake the new one.

Local farmers consented to donate some of their land for the day for parking purposes and Fred and Edward Bates allowed Norman Park to again be the centre of the day's festivities. Indeed this was reported in the *Huddersfield Examiner*:

'Not Again' he said.

It's no good pretending that some Denby Dale folk haven't been a little worried about this 'ere pie. One can visualise for instance just how farmer, Edward Bates, of Inkerman Farm, is feeling as he milks his cows this afternoon, while in the big field behind his mistal, the pie makes its triumphal entry. There was a crowd of around 80,000 jammed into that same field when the 1928 event took place. It was reported that the farmer at Inkerman was heard to exclaim 'never again' at the height of all the commotion. But the pie is here again and farmer Bates, like his predecessor, has agreed to loan his field to the Pie Committee… it's the only one big enough.

The local farmers were consulted as to the best time in the farming year to hold the event and September was the date agreed upon, when most crops would be cleared. The services of 2,000 men to patrol the crowd and the traffic, which was expected to arrive from all directions, were engaged. Also involved in the day were the police, army and civil defence volunteers along with 200 volunteers from Wakefield, Huddersfield and Barnsley. Police scouts, sea scouts and boy scouts were to arrive on the following day to clear all the litter, for which the local farmers had agreed to provide trailers to cart away. David Brown Tractors Ltd offered the services of their demonstration team for the day itself and afterwards to plough and restore all the land used on the Saturday. In addition the largest dry stone walling contractors in the district promised to rebuild any damaged walls.

To keep the local public up to date with these developments a newsletter was produced, informing them of schedules and entertainments, these letters were always signed by 'Pie Man'.

Of course, the committee also required money. To this end many fundraising events were organised by the Entertainments Committee:

From Pie News – July 1964:

They say that hard work never killed anyone, well this committee has proved that to be quite true. They were given the task of raising £1,250, this and much more has been raised with a programme of events which [sic] has been varied to give every type of entertainment possible in our village. They started the ball rolling with a whist drive which made about £7, next came a coffee morning at the home of Mrs G Naylor, here we notched up another £60. Things just snowballed from then on, we went on to make £500 at the traction engine rally, £250 at the dance which we had in a garage at Shepley. The only disappointment the committee have had was the last event, the gala. I don't think worse weather could have been ordered and it spoiled what had promised to be the highlight of the past year's labours.

Pie Day is almost here, just another week to go. What a day it promises to be. If you just stop and think for a moment, we are doing something which nowhere in the world has been attempted. The world will know about it come September 5th, and whilst you are just thinking, "What am I doing to ensure that this day goes down in history as a success?" There are lots of jobs for you to help with, even if you can only spare us half an hour. After all, it's only one day in every thirty years or so that this event comes along.

Can you imagine this event coming up again in thirty years time. I am sure the younger generation will be capable of doing the job, but will it be a pie as we know it today, or will it be made in the form of a giant Meat and Potatoe PILL, taken with a glass of 'Jubilee' or whatever else you fancy. So come along and give a hand, everybody welcome, whatever sex, providing you have a pair of hands. You only have to give your name to any committee member, or to call in at the Pie Office, which is up High Street, next to Kitson's Office.

Everything is going according to plan and the Committee together with Youth Club members and friends, are busy sorting out the ton of bunting which has arrived, and then they hope to start erecting it about a week before Pie Day. So if you see young people hanging from lamp posts don't rush off and report them for vandalism. The Fairy Lights are soon to arrive, a convoy of lorries has already been to Sheffield to collect the four large stars which are to hang on the viaducts.

Don't forget this house decoration Competition, it is open to all houses regardless of whether they are on the Pie route or not. Also the prize has been increased so get stuck in and lets have a good show

1st. Prize Silver casket full of Cigarettes and £5

2nd. Prize 50 Cigarettes and £3

3rd. Prize 25 Cigarettes and £2

Prizes have been donated by Messrs. Gallagher, makers of Senior Service Cigarettes.

If you or your neighbours fancy having a float in the procession come along, but most of all, don't forget the children, they love to get dressed up, let's have a bigger turnout than at our washed out Carnival. Two lorries will pick up all the children outside the School at 1-15 p.m. Prizes will be given to the winners of the different age groups. Prizes of £5, £3, and £2 (Given to us by Messrs. W. D. & H. O. Wills) will be given for the best floats.

CATERING COMMITTEE

This committee of local ladies are raring to tackle the Pie serving job, they should prove to be the fittest amongst us, having had to pass the M.O.H. tests before they can go near the Pie. This, coupled with a training diet of Milk Stout & Eggs should see them through the rigours of the day. The husbands of these good ladies Should not expect to see pie served up for dinner for a long time after Sept. 5th.

SALES COMMITTEE

Have you bought your Pie plate, and one for your friends yet? If not, don't leave it too late. As things are working out, it is possible that you may be disappointed if you leave it till Pie day before buying one. The Pottery have told the committee, in reply to their request for further stocks of plates, that they are unable to produce any more before Pie day, and it is the general policy that once Sept. 5th is over no more will be ordered, otherwise this job of selling could go on for ever. The Despatching Dept. are at present getting off an order for 750 plates. The company who has ordered these will send them out to their own customers throughout the world and attached to each one will be a calander for 1965.

If you have ordered one of the special hand made tankards or if you would like to go along to the Post Office where you can choose the one you like at no extra charge.

Lewis Craven & Co. Ltd., Printers & Stationers, Denby Dale.

PLANNING COMMITTEE

The programme of entertainments for Pie day is now complete, and what a list it is. I should think that it is impossible to see everything that is happening throughout the day. Just to give you some idea of what you can see:-

Brass Bands Denby Dale, Thurlstone, Old Silkstone, Duke of Wellingtons (W.R. Batt.) W.R. Fire Service, Hazley Mansford Pipe Band, No. 1 Regional Band of the R.A.F.

Displays of all kinds can be seen in the Show Ring, which is where the Traction Engine Rally was held, and also up Miller Hill.

Professional Wrestling from 12 noon to 2 p.m This is to be in a marquee, next to the Show Ring, giving you a top class programme.

A **Concert** will be held in the same Marquee during the evening 6 p.m. to 7-30 p.m.

Firework Display 8-45 p m. so don't put the children to bed too early.

To round off the day, we have of course, the Dance which is to be held in the Garage at Sovereign again. With music (to some) provided by the Swinging Blue Jeans, the Terry Lightfoot Band and supporting group.

Tickets for all these events can be obtained from the Pie Office. You can also buy a Brochure containing a full programme of events.

CONSTRUCTION COMMITTEE

The barn at Dry Hill is coming along nicely. It's looking more like a fit place to bake a Pie. It has, of course, to come up to a very high standard of cleanliness in order to pass the M.O.H regulations and when the preparation and baking are in progress a security system on a par to any in force at these government departments will be mounted, in order to keep out spies and unhealthy bacteria. if you want a chance to see inside this place, all you have to do is come along and help on Pie day and help, because, as promised, the week after the Pie a Barn Dance is being organised, with supper of course, laid on. This will be open to all the people who have helped in any way over the last twelve months.

One more job which this committee have to do is the fixing up of decorations under the viaducts which span the two main roads. The Daily Mail are also having a large banner put up there. Only brave and well insured men need apply for this task.

The last item of our News Letter could be called the "Rumour Scotching" column. Lots of rumours are circulating around the village just now. Some are true, but mostly they are just a lot of hot air broadcast by the Pie Knockers, so don't take too much notice of all the stories you hear. If in doubt, call at the Pie Office they will do the best they can to put you right.

This trip to London which has been promised to the helpers is not fixed as some would have you believe. All the names are to go into a hat and the lucky ones picked out. The other people who are going to London are going to work, and it's jolly hard work too, they will be on the Pie stand at the Food Fair ten hours a day. So who can begrudge them the price of bed and breakfast while they are working.

Such a lot of people have also got the idea that the police are going to stop cars coming into the village on Pie Day. This is not true of course, but they will stop them parking where they may cause an obstruction.

Congratulations to Mr. G. Naylor on his fine looking oven, quite an advance has been made since the 1928 days. The magnificent traction engine which is to pull the Pie has arrived in the village, but is under lock and key, waiting to tackle this important task. It should be a proud day for its owners.

Pie-Man

An example of 'Pie News' from August 1964.

Front page of the Steam Traction Engine Rally programme.

An offer to subscribe to the Denby Dale pie fund and receive benefits.

Gala Day advertisement, 6 June 1964.

EVENTS

SUNDAY. MARCH 29th :

2-00 Opening Ceremony

SUNDAY, MARCH 29th & MONDAY, MARCH 30th

2-10 Grand Parade

2-40 Obstacle Race for Traction Engines

3-15 Obstacle Race for Steam Waggons

3-45 Back to Back Race

4-15 Musical Chairs

4-45 Ladies' Invitation Race

5-15 Final Parade and Presentation of Prizes

ACKNOWLEDGEMENTS

The Entertainments Committee wish to thank all those who have helped in the Rally arrangements and especially:

Mr. S. C. Butler of the South Yorkshire Traction Engine Club

Mr. B. E. Kitson for the Fields

The Police, the A.A., the St. John Ambulance Brigade

Wakefield Motor Club

Owners and Crews of Engines, Veteran and Vintage Cars

Youth Club Members

Prizes Donated by

J. Canning Ltd.—Tyre Distributors

Wm. Shaw & Sons (Huddersfield) Ltd.
Industrial & Domestic Fuel Distributors

Benjamin Shaw & Sons Ltd.—Soft Drink Manufacturers

Redex Ltd.—Lubricant Manufacturers

other prizes received too late to mention

Fuel for the Rally supplied by
S. Haigh & Son, Wakefield Road, Denby Dale

ENGINES

No.	Owner	Make	Eng. No.	Year	Reg. No.
1.	M. BREWER Huntgate Pickering	Robey 'Village Queen'	33957	1922	FE5043

Acquired for preservation 1962. Attended Rallies 1963, since had a complete overhaul.

2.	FEARNLEYS Castleford	Fowler 'Tiger'	14406	1917	CJ4338

3.	F. N. DEAN Airedale Castleford	Fowler	15732	1922	PT832

Only recently acquired by present owner.

4.	J. HARDY Church Street Ulleskelf	Fowler	9381	1902	

Built for John Smiths Brewery Tadcaster. Sold to Fearnley's of Castleford. Then to Johnston's the Showmen, again sold to Baker's of Kellington for thrashing, acquired for preservation in 1963.

5.	DICKENSON & Sons (Emley) Ltd. Doncaster	Burrell	4070	1927	WW2181

One of the last Steam Rollers built by Chas. Burrell of Thetford.

6.	H. PARKIN Cutsyke Castleford	Foden	12364	1926	TW4207

This waggon was used for tarspraying for many years and was acquired for preservation in 1963.

Details of the steam rally events inside the programme.

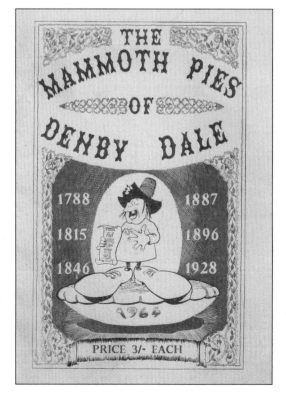

Front cover of Nora Kitson's pie history booklet.

100

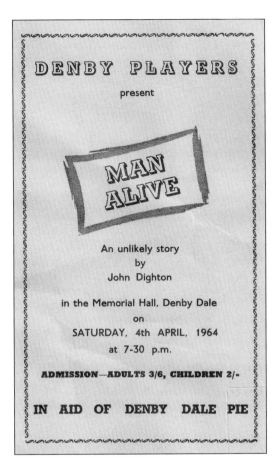

The Denby Dale Players repertory company put on a play to raise funds for the 1964 pie.

Cast, crew and play synopsis of 'Man Alive' performed in April 1964 by the Denby Dale players.

Cast

(in order of their appearance)

Waldorf	Gerald Kaye
Belgravia	Ruth Walker
George Ingle	Arthur Crossland
Daphne Jameson	Avril Ryan
Miss Yates	Nellie Harrop
Oakshott	Sally Waldie
Jubilee	Susan Longbottom
Mr. Wembley	Jack Jones
Mr. Hathaway	Edward Hinchliffe
Messenger Boy	Rodney Oakes
Fred	Chris Herbert
Miss Butterworth	Susan Wilson
Miss Adshead	Shirley Herbert
The Police Commissioner	Fred Barden

Lighting	Leonard Hardcastle
Stage Management and Effects	Ralph Harvey and Bob Ryan
Continuity	Gillian Keeling

PRODUCED BY JUDITH BARDEN

Synopsis of Scenes

ACT I

The morning of New Year's Day

ACT II

Half an hour later

ACT III

Half an hour later

Time—the present

The action of the play passes in a window of Hathaway's Department Store in Oxford Street, London.

The members of the cast wish to extend thanks to all who have helped in any way in this production and to those who have given encouragement by their support. We especially wish to thank the Scissett Amateur Operatic Society who have most kindly loaned scenery and many props.

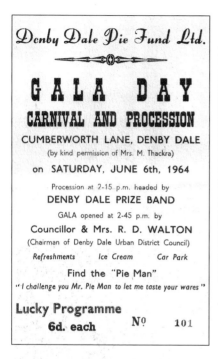

Denby Dale Pie Fund Ltd.

GALA DAY

CARNIVAL AND PROCESSION

CUMBERWORTH LANE, DENBY DALE

(by kind permission of Mrs. M. Thackra)

on SATURDAY, JUNE 6th, 1964

Procession at 2-15 p.m. headed by
DENBY DALE PRIZE BAND

GALA opened at 2-45 p.m. by

Councillor & Mrs. R. D. WALTON

(Chairman of Denby Dale Urban District Council)

Refreshments   Ice Cream   Car Park

Find the "Pie Man"

" I challenge you Mr. Pie Man to let me taste your wares "

Lucky Programme
6d. each   Nº   101

PROGRAMME OF EVENTS

p.m. (approx.)

1-45   Judging of Fancy Dress and Floats

2-15   Procession moves off led by Denby Dale Prize Band

2-45   Gala Opening and Presentation of Prizes by Councillor and Mrs. R. D. Walton Chairman of D.D.U.C.

3-00   Five-a-side Football Referee Mr. A. Holland (of Barnsley)

3-30   Display by the Skelmanthorpe Fire Bgde.

p.m. (approx.)

4-00   Five-a-side Football

4-30   Display by the Barnsley Company of the Hallamshire Battalion York and Lancaster Regiment (T.A.)

5-00   Five-a-side Football (Finals)

5-30   Display of driving by the Wakefield & Dist. Motor Sports Club

6-00   Selections by the Denby Dale Prize Band

Events timetable listed in the Gala Day programme.

Gala Day programme 1964.

Other activities included a children's party, two motor rallies, a bonfire and barbecue, and Nora Kitson's booklet *The Mammoth Pies of Denby Dale* celebrated the successes and disasters of previous occasions. Thousands of pie plates were also made in 1964 and were stored in the barn of Mr Alfred George, whose delivery van also became a pie plate delivery service. A fashion show was also held at the Victoria Memorial Hall on 4 December 1963 attended by around 400 people:

> *The collection was shown by Constance Darwin of High Street, Huddersfield. Leading a line-up of professional models were international mannequins Susan Greenwood and Tessa Stanley. Susan, a Denby Dale girl, was one of the first to dare the 'plunge line'. Susan Platt, wife of Yorkshire cricketer, Bob Platt who lives at Holmfirth and Fiona Batt, who is married to Yorkshire socialite Jimmy Batt, were also amongst the models.*

Also included in the evening's entertainment were the prizes awarded in the Denby Dale pie plate design competition held recently, which were presented by Huddersfield born athlete, Derek Ibbotson. Ibbotson set the world record for running a mile in 1957 at 3 minutes 57.2 seconds.

Luckily for the committee, a Denby Dale pie was an excellent marketing opportunity for local businesses and the following items were donated:

The pie dish, which measured 18 feet by 6 feet by 18 inches deep, was made at Aireworth Engineering Co Ltd, Otley, where chairman of the Pie & Contents Committee, Brian Kitson was managing director. The Kitson family of Denby Dale was steeped with involvement in the Pies.

Fashion Show

by courtesy of

CONSTANCE DARWIN

of High Street, Huddersfield

MEMORIAL HALL
DENBY DALE
HUDDERSFIELD

WEDNESDAY
DECEMBER 4th
1963

at 8-00 p.m.

Light Refreshments

Admission 4/-

Proceeds to the
Denby Dale Pie Fund

Advertising card for the fashion show.

The awards for the pie plate design competition being given out. Left to right: Margaret Sowerby (3rd), Derek Ibbotson, Mel Ryan (Yorkshire cricketer), Thomas Smith (1st), Mrs Ibbotson, D S Pearson (2nd).

Brian's grandfather, Joe Kitson, supplied the 8,000 bricks required to build the 1887 pie oven and served on the 1896 pie. They also supplied the bricks for constructing the oven in 1928. George Naylor of the Naylor Brothers Group in Denby Dale constructed this year's oven, thereby keeping his family's record of involvement in the pies intact.

The Yorkshire Electricity Board supplied the power, the Daily Mail provided £300 worth of meat, Job Earnshaw & Brothers, farmers of West Cumberland, supplied the potatoes, Stafford Allen & Sons gave the spices, J H Green of Denby Dale and Samuel Drake & Sons supplied the flour and so the list goes on.

Another tradition that began in 1964 was that of local school children planting a field of potatoes to be used in the pie. A tractor was loaned by the David Brown Corporation to plough a field on the outskirts of the village and to take a mixed load of seed potatoes given by the West Cumberland Farmers Ltd and a trailer-load of young children to plant them.

The pie dish and oven at Naylor Brothers, Cawthorne.
(Susan Buckley collection.)

The pie oven, about to leave the premises of Naylor Brothers in Cawthorne.
(Huddersfield Examiner/Tolson Museum.)

In order to maximise publicity, large signboards were erected around the village to inform passing motorists and the general public of the forthcoming event. One was sited on Cumberworth Road, one on Wakefield Road and one at the Dunkirk on the Barnsley Road.

The notices, all of them the work of Shepley born sign-writer Harold Copley, show the pie with a rich golden crust and Denby Dale viaduct against a yellow background. The lettering is in blue and the panel at the foot of the board announcing the pie to be the world's biggest is in red. The dimensions of the boards are 6 feet x 4 feet. Mr Copley said the design for the notices was first drawn up, not on paper but on the bar of the Junction Inn (now the Dunkirk). The Pie Committee liked what they saw and very soon afterwards Mr Copley was hard at work with his brushes in the cellar of the home of the pies secretary, Mrs S Turton. Mr Copley's work on behalf of the pie is by no means over. Underway he has two more signs – one showing a big slice of the pie, which is to be erected in the field where the event is to be held, and another bearing the words 'Pie News', which is to head a noticeboard in the village on which will be posted details of coming events in connection with the pie. Although Mr Copley thinks that the pie project is assuming 'terrifying proportions', he's not worried. His home at 3 Inkerman Cottage overlooks the field where the pie is to be cooked and so he's sure of a grandstand view on the big day.

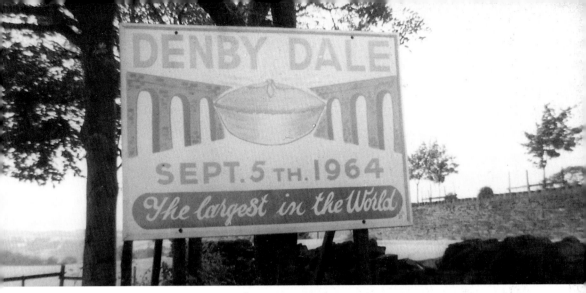

One of the advertising sign boards created by Harold Copley.

Harold Copley, pictured next to his handiwork.

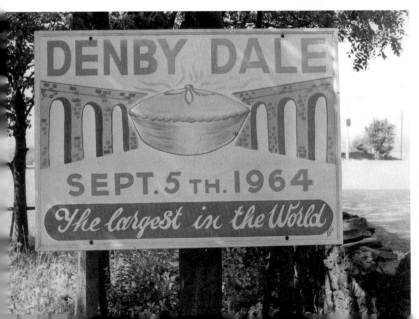

A closer view of Mr Copley's work. *(West Yorkshire Archives/Tolson Museum.)*

Baking the pie itself was the most important consideration of all. Head chef George Saville and his fellow cooks and butchers had the problem of creating the monster from 3 tons of beef, 1½ tons of potatoes, and ½ ton of gravy and seasoning. There was also ½ ton of flour and ¼ ton of lard (the flour and lard being required for 650 square feet of crust). The cooks were: Brian Kitson, Trevor Senior, Dennis Hargreaves, William Wordsworth, Edward Hudson, Peter Holmes, David Goodwin, Frank Hobson, Joseph Kay, George Saville and Alan Cooper.

Hector Buckley's newly built 50 feet by 90 feet milking parlour at Dry Hill, Lower Denby became the hub of cooking operation. Inside was a giant mobile oven, twenty-five 3kwt boilers (each capable of pre-cooking 50lbs of meat at a time) and 4,100 cubic feet of refrigerators in which the meat was to be stored from the Wednesday preceding pie weekend. There were also one dozen chopping blocks, two large dairy tanks for sterilising knives and a tank containing 300 gallons of fresh water. The team of butchers, all from the Denby Dale area, took 100 man-hours to cut 4,500lbs of beef into 1-inch cubes. Ideal simmering temperature was 150 degrees Fahrenheit and six needle thermometers buried deep in the steaming meat and potato were constantly monitoring the cooking process. The butchers had to keep the twenty-five boilers stoked with steaming beef and seasoning. Each load of meat was given a two-hour 'turn' before being transferred from the oven into the pie dish. The potatoes were also pre-cooked and were the last ingredient into the pie before the 7 feet x 2 feet slabs of pastry were laid on top. Every so often the juices in the boilers were drained off to be used to make the 100 gallons of gravy.

Because the pie was being cooked at Lower Denby the steep gradient of Miller Hill would have to be negotiated during the pie's processional route. This was solved by dividing the dish into sections that were individually covered with plates. The other main problem was the Public

The men who cooked the 1964 pie. Left to right: Brian Kitson, Trevor Senior, Dennis Hargreaves, William Wordsworth, Edward Hudson, Peter Holmes, David Goodwin, Frank Hobson, Joseph Kay, George Saville and Alan Cooper.

The pie oven arrives at the Dunkirk, Lower Denby. *(Huddersfield Examiner/Tolson Museum.)*

Butchers' knives at the ready the cooks pose for a publicity still.

The Pie oven, entering Hector Buckley's barn. *(Susan Buckley collection.)*

Final checks are made on the oven. *(Susan Buckley collection.)*

The scene for the great bake is set. *(Susan Buckley collection.)*

With health and safety paramount, no part of the dish is left uncleaned.

(Susan Buckley collection.)

109

Work begins on cutting the beef into 1 inch cubes. Included in the photograph are Joseph Kaye, far left, Edward Hudson, in the stripes at the far end of the table, and Peter Fretwell, second from the right. *(Susan Buckley collection.)*

It took 100 man hours to prepare the meat for cooking. *(Susan Buckley collection.)*

Pastry squares being prepared in the barn at Dry Hill. *(Susan Buckley collection.)*

Health Inspector. All the cooks had to have medical checks to prove their suitability and conditions in the milking parlour were kept totally sterile. The trailer on to which the pie was to be placed would be towed by the traction engine *Marshal Foch*, owned by the Hunt family company, Specialoid Pistons. This was a two-man job, entrusted to experts Tony Hunt (steering) and Bert Baker (steam power and breaking).

The stringent health and safety regulations caused no end of anxiety amongst the cooks but a local man, Mr Raymond Haigh of Upper Denby, did redress the balance a little.

The Marshal Foch, pulling the pie oven tests the gradient of Miller Hill. *(Huddersfield Examiner/Tolson Museum.)*

Mr Haigh, a coalman of impressive stature, was on sentry duty at the door of the milking parlour where he refused the Public Health officials entry when they came to inspect the pie whilst it was baking. Unlike the cooks, the inspectors had not been subject to any medical and therefore were not able to prove their cleanliness.

In Raymond's own words (taken from a documentary broadcast on *Radio Leeds* in 1988):

I started at teatime, Friday night, and I was in charge. I had a list of twenty-two names, twenty-two people who were allowed into the place where they were actually baking the pie, and no other person was allowed in. In those days they called this area Denby Dale Urban District Council, it wasn't under Kirklees then and they had their own Public Health Inspector called Mr Urmstone. On Saturday morning, two big, posh cars rolled up and two gentlemen got out of these cars and met Mr Urmstone who brought them to the door and introduced me to them. Both were Chief Public Health Inspectors and had come to see that things were going right.

I said, 'Oh yes, just a minute Mr Urmstone,' so I got my list. I knew Mr Urmstone's name was on the list of course. I said, 'now, what are your names gentlemen?' and they told me and I said, 'well . . . you're not on my list, so you can't come in.

Mr Urmstone said, 'I know Raymond, but they are Chief Public Health Inspectors'.

I replied, 'oh are they – yes – well, THEY ARE NOT ON MY LIST SO THEY CAN'T COME IN.'

And they'd to jump back in their big posh cars and go!

Raymond was well-suited to his post. He had spent two years in the Coldstream Guards.

I've done Buckingham Palace and Windsor Castle so that's probably a little bit of experience. Bit different though, guarding the king to guarding a Denby Dale pie.

Born in 1929 in Skelmanthorpe, Raymond's family moved to Denby Dale when he was only a few months old. He left school when he was fourteen to work as a cloth-finisher in one of the local mills. National Service took him into the Coldstream Guards, where he met King George VI, who said good morning to him. He began his own business in 1959 as a coal merchant and continued with this until he retired. Married to Ina, the couple had four children and six grandchildren.

For the day to be a success an enormous amount of publicity was required, before the committee had even been formed Mrs Kitson had been interviewed on television regarding her intentions to bake another pie. Press releases were despatched instigating calls from national newspapers and then Frank Dale of the popular BBC programme, *Tonight* came to the village. The resulting film (made in November 1963) took two days to shoot, lasted nearly a quarter of an hour and included footage from Brian Kitson's engineering works where welding was taking place on the dish itself. Fyfe Robertson provided the commentary for the film although his car ended up in the wars somewhat.

From the Souvenir Brochure 1964, by John Netherwood:

In the course of the film Fyfe Robertson tasted some pie from a 20lbs miniature baked by George Saville at his shop in Upper Denby. Afterwards we all sat down in the George Inn across the road to eat this massive miniature. Whilst we were eating someone came in to ask if the owner of a new white Ford Consul would move his motorcar. This car turned out to belong to Fyfe Robertson himself. Not wishing to disturb his meal, one of us 'Dalers' (who shall remain nameless) offered to move the car for him. Unfortunately the brewery wagon had just been delivering barrels of ale and had left the planks off the cellarway. Down went the Robertson Consul. The unfortunate driver now has the title of 'im as put Fyfe Robertson's motor down't beer ole'.

Fyfe Robertson (1902 – 1987) was a Scottish television journalist. After briefly studying medicine at Glasgow University, he became a reporter firstly with the *Glasgow Herald* and later in London with the *Daily Herald, Daily Express* and *Picture Post* magazine. When *Picture Post* closed in 1957 he went to work in television. He is chiefly remembered for his association with the BBC programme *Tonight*. His bearded, haggard face topped by a tweed trilby hat and a slow over-emphatic Scottish voice became well known. For *Tonight* Robertson travelled widely providing serious stories as well as finding some remarkable eccentrics. When *Tonight* was replaced by *24 Hours*, Robertson continued in his same investigative manner. Despite being a heavy smoker, he remained in good health and whilst in his late sixties he took part in two exhausting televised expeditions, across the Scottish Highlands on horseback and paddling down the Severn in a canoe. He died in Eastbourne in 1987.

John Netherwood continues:

When Frank Dale left us (after his initial visit) he had in mind some seven or eight minutes running time, In my ignorance I had imagined that such a film could be shot in half a day. How wrong I was. On the first morning we all turned up at nine o'clock sharp in John Hinchliffe's billiard room where a large number of photographers and pie relics had been got together and laid out on the billiard table. This room was to be the headquarters throughout the filming. At midnight the same day, after a short lunch break, the team were still hard at it in Brian Kitson's Otley engineering works, where they shot the welding of the great pie dish at midnight. They sat down to their evening meal at Brian Kitson's home in Ilkley at one-thirty in the morning and at nine thirty on the following day they were back in the billiard room ready for another day's work. They left us at ten-thirty on the second night and set off for York where they were to shoot another film the following day. The film that resulted from all this work lasted for nearly a quarter of an hour, a most unusual length for that particular programme. Such was the favourable reception of this film that it was repeated on Boxing Day (1963).

The *Tonight* programme opened with a short fanfare before Fyfe Robertson was pictured speaking to camera on Wakefield Road, overlooking Springfield Mill. The premises of Kenyon's and Naylor's were also briefly featured. A potted history of the pies then followed, beginning with 1788. Fyfe Robertson's next piece to camera was in Cliff Style Field where he suggests that the only article to have survived from this earliest of pies is a gravy-stained apron, which was briefly shown. Film of the corn mill at the bottom of Miller Hill was then followed by Fyfe doing his third piece to camera at Cuckstool Farm, complete with two farmers and a border collie. The fourth piece to camera was filmed at the burial site of the 1887 pie at Toby Wood being followed with film of the railway station. Old photographs of 1896 and 1928 cover these pies before the fifth piece to camera saw Fyfe back on Wakefield Road above the premises of Z Hinchliffe in the shadow of the viaduct. The history completed the film moved on to the 1964 pie preparations.

Beginning with Denby Dale Band practising for the pie parade in the band hut on Hillside. Interspersed with the band were scenes involving Hector Buckley and John Hinchliffe discussing the meat, Hector Buckley in his barn which was being prepared for the arrival of the oven, and the welding and construction of the pie dish at Otley. The programme culminated with an interview with George Saville (head chef in charge of the pie) in his butcher's shop at Upper House, Upper Denby. He talked about the pressure of baking the pie and the importance of the gravy. He finally granted Fyfe a chance to taste the pie recipe by taking a 20lbs trial pie out of the oven. The programme finished with the credits playing over film of Denby Dale Band practising again. Although its initial broadcast was delayed by the assassination of American President John F Kennedy, the film set the ball

George Saville with Fyfe Robertson at the butcher's shop in Upper Denby.

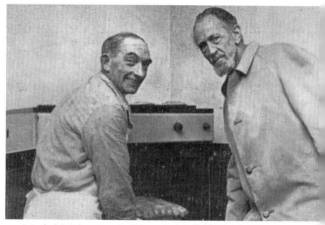

rolling. Press cutting survive coming from many countryies, including the *Montreal Star*, dated Thursday 31 December 1963, the headline was *Biggest Pie of all Time To Be Made In Yorkshire*, and information was even requested by Teheran.

In May a publicity stunt was set up on the Calder and Hebble Navigation Canal outside the Ship Inn at Mirfield. The pie dish was launched onto the water and was due to complete the last stage of its journey from Otley (where it was made) to Huddersfield under the power of its own 5hp outboard motor. Its crew consisted of Captain Brian Kitson along with publicity officer, John Netherwood and ten girls, eight in cocktail dresses and two in Swiss naval uniforms. Seventy-three newspapermen from all over the country turned up to see the event. Later that night the dish was sunk by persons unknown, which, although having nothing to do with the publicity committee, still made headlines, particularly so when Lloyds, who had insured the dish under a marine accidents policy paid for the salvage operation.

All aboard the pie dish outside the Ship Inn at Mirfield.

The dish being towed along the Calder & Hebble Navigation Canal.

As with other water craft, the pie dish had to negotiate the locks on the canal.

115

Eventually the committee had to employ a public relations firm as the work was becoming too much for them. The final event involved the tasting of four pie recipes, each containing a different seasoning, in order to select the one that would be used on the real thing. A group of distinguished experts including Harold Taylor, Catherine Floris, Christopher Floris (director of Floris Bakeries, who made birthday cakes for Winston Churchill), Robert Stafford and the celebrities Clement Freud and Philip Harben were invited to pass judgement. Philip Harben (1906 – 1970) was an English cook, recognised as the first TV celebrity chef. He presented a BBC wireless cooking programme from 1942 and BBC TV programmes *Cookery* from 1946 to 1951, then *Cookery Lesson* and *What's Cooking* from 1956. He had a regular column in the British *Woman's Own* magazine in the 1950s. He also appeared as himself in two films, *Mr Lucifer* (1953) and the 1955 Norman Wisdom vehicle *Man of the Moment,* instantly recognisable by his educated accent, expansive manner, ample girth and neatly trimmed beard.

At the George Hotel in Huddersfield the experts met and tasted four different pies eventually and unanimously pronounced that the best-tasting combination of spices was number FD895, though the recipe is kept a village secret.

Clement Freud who acted as chairman for the judges declared:

Although we had been told that all the pies had in them a secret ingredient, all the pies lacked the ingredient of sufficient salt.

Head cook George Saville expressed surprise at Mr Freud's comments on the salt. He said:

We did not put any salt in. We left it to the specialists who provided the seasoning. But I can assure you there will be plenty of salt in the mammoth pie.

TV Cook Phillip Harben said that coming from London he found the pies dull. Did he think that the final enormous Denby Dale pie would be better?

It's a pious hope' he said.

Clement Freud added:

When the 30,000 people come to eat it, they can blame us collectively, our individual reputations will remain intact.

Hopes of a profit of £25,000 were high. Estimates of possible crowds ranged from 90,000 to 250,000 though these proved to be highly wild and probably deterred some people from coming, but after so much hard work and with so much achieved the outlook was positive . . . then tragedy struck.

From the *Sheffield Telegraph* dated 1 September 1964:

The world famous Denby Dale pie ceremony will go on as planned on Saturday in spite of an accident which [sic] killed four of the main organisers. Press officer Mr John Netherwood said 'The pie day celebrations will go ahead. When we heard the news we visited all the relatives of the four dead men and asked them whether they thought the celebrations should be cancelled. But in each and every case the relatives said the event should still be held.'

DENBY DALE PIE

Mid Summer
BUFFET DANCE

George Hotel, Huddersfield, July 16th

*To meet the Gourmets and food experts who are
tasting recipes for the 1964 Pie*

Dinner Jackets   **8-30 p.m. Bar till 1 a.m.**

A ticket for the pie tasting
event at the George Hotel
in Huddersfield.

Phillip Harben prepares to serve portions of the four
different trial pies. Left to right: Harold Taylor, Catherine
Floris, Christopher Floris, Clement Freud, Robert
Stafford.

Phillip Harben gets stuck
into his work.

Christopher Floris and
Clement Freud on the left
watch as Phillip Harben
uses the ceremonial
carvers to fill the plates.

News of the fatal crash stunned the bunting- and flag-decorated Yorkshire village and Union Jacks flew at half-mast above the wool mill chimneys.

Black Monday in the Village

Four members of the pie organisation were instantly killed in a road crash near Grantham whilst returning from ITV Studios, Teddington, near London, where they had travelled to take part in a programme featuring the pie of 1964 for possible use in a new Eammon Andrews show. The recording had ended at 2am on Monday morning and the four men were being driven by John Haigh in a Sunbeam Rapier back up the M1 to Yorkshire. The accident occurred at Grantham bypass at Little Ponton when the tailboard of a 16 ton articulated lorry collided with the car, death was instant. The men were:

Benny Beever, Laurence Wainwright and George Saville, tragically killed in the accident.

Benjamin (Benny) Beever (eighty-six years old) of Ivy Bank, Ingbirchworth Mr Beever was the head of a well-known firm of builders. He had eight sons and a daughter and twenty-three grandchildren. Mr Beever retired from business several years ago and left the running of it to his sons. Only a month before his death he had invited the entire village of Ingbirchworth to his eighty-sixth birthday party at his home and nearly 200 turned up. He was acting as an advisor to the pie committee and had attended the 1887, 1896 and 1928 Pies.

John Schofield Haigh, the fourth victim of the accident, and his wife, Pat, pictured on their wedding day in 1963.

George Saville (fifty-two years old). Sitting in the back seat of the car, he was the leading baker of the 1964 pie. After six years as an army cook he returned home and built up a butchery business at Upper Denby and was one of the first to take up the challenge of baking the new pie. He was involved in the Tonight *programme for BBC TV, being interviewed on camera by Fyfe Robertson. Mr Saville, of Upper House, left a widow and a fifteen-year-old daughter Jeanette. Mr Saville was in charge of the cooks preparing the pie and also the baker of the miniature pies from which the ingredients were chosen.*

Lawrence Wainwright (sixty-three years old)
Mr Wainwright's interests were very much involved with Denby Dale Brass Band. He played

in the 1928 procession and was no doubt looking forward to doing the same again in 1964. He was employed by Z Hinchliffe and Sons for over fifty years. A widower, he lived at Springfield Houses in Denby Dale and left a daughter.

John Schofield Haigh (twenty-four years old)
The driver of the tragedy, only twenty-four years old, he only undertook the trip when another member of the committee was unable to go. He lived at Eastfield House (formerly Highfield House), Kitchenroyd with his wife Patricia (who was due to give birth to the couple's first child soon after the tragedy). Mr Haigh was chairman of the Pie Planning Committee.

Mr Raymond Haigh, who drove the lorry carrying the pie dish, didn't know of the tragedy until he reached Denby Dale. Mr Sidney Turton and his wife Monica, who is secretary to the Pie Committee, also passed the crash in their car.

The mood of the village was captured in a newspaper article dated 2 September:

Outwardly the villagers look and act as they did this time last week and up to Monday morning. It is not an easy part to play. For behind this surface barrier of traditional Yorkshire cheeriness, behind the flags and the bunting and coloured lights that decorate the narrow streets, behind the posters and hoardings that invite outsiders to come and see the world's biggest pie, Denby Dale is in mourning. Many tears have been shed behind the closed curtains of Denby Dale, for in a closely-knit village like this there are bonds of friendship and loyalty between all. Visitors to the village will detect none of the anguish and horror felt by the locals because in true tradition of showmanship, the show will go on. But that will be on Saturday. Until then Denby Dale will remain stunned. Today a cool wind whipped around the squat weather-worn houses and along the near-deserted main street. Here and there little knots of women in aprons and workmen on their way to the local mill stood talking of the tragedy. It was the one topic of conversation in the pubs and clubs and factories and mills. Above the big mill in the village, where one of the dead men, Mr Lawrence Wainwright, worked, a flag fluttered in the breeze at half-mast. At the nearby Denby Dale and Cumberworth railway station the lone porter summed it all up: 'Most of the heart has gone out of the job. But just wait until Saturday. We'll be back to normal and will give all those people who are coming a day to remember.'

The big day approached and many of the houses in the village and along the route of the procession were decorated, even the viaduct was trimmed with illuminations under the supervision of Jane Beavers. A report in the local newspaper commented in wry style that Morecambe invested £125,000 and Blackpool £500,000 on their illuminations and that Denby Dale had paid out the princely sum of £56 10s. The railway line, which was due to have been closed down three months before the advent of the pie, had been kept open and would remain open for four days after the end of the proceedings. A subject recorded by the *Huddersfield Examiner*:

High Street, Wakefield Road, the flags and bunting flutter in the light breeze. A delivery of coal has also just been made. *(West Yorkshire Archives/Tolson Museum.)*

A village in waiting, Kitson's premises can be seen to the left.

(West Yorkshire Archives/Tolson Museum.)

The platform, on which the pie was to be ceremonially opened and served from under construction. *(Huddersfield Examiner/Tolson Museum.)*

The serving tables are positioned around the pie platform in Norman Park in readiness for the great **day.** *(Susan Buckley collection.)*

Beeching's Finger & the Pie
Had Dr. Beeching had his way, the village might have been seeing its last train in three days
time. Even now this could be a swansong occasion for Denby Dale's little station. September
7 – just two days hence – was to have been the day of the Penistone line's closure according
to a British Railways Board public notice last March. But for the moment the death sentence
hangs fire pending the Minister of Transport's consideration of some eighty-seven objections.
The pie means that the booking office at Denby Dale station will be open for the first time in
two years.

The night before pie day (4 September) the *Huddersfield Examiner* recorded a final flurry of
nerves:

Extra Pastry Needed
There was drama in Denby Dale last night as organisers suddenly realised that there would not
be enough crust to go round. They appealed for local bakers to make nearly half a mile of pastry.
Mrs Beryl Holden, one of the pie publicity officers explained: The problem is that although the
pie itself is deep we can only have one layer of crust on top and that isn't nearly enough, so we
planned to bake a lot extra.'

The women of the village rallied round and saved the day. The main cooking process began
at Dry Hill, where the curious could, for a nominal fee, climb a gantry and peer through the
windows of the milking parlour to see the ingredients, cooking process and, no doubt, smell
the creation of the giant pie. More than 3,000 people paid 1s for this opportunity to watch
the eighteen cooks in action. The death of George Saville had robbed the cooking team of
its leader, so local butcher, Jack Hirst was called in at the last minute to take over as head
chef.

Yorkshire Evening Post – 4 September 1964:

Well, it smells champion! From the steamy depths of farmer Hector Buckley's barn on the
outskirts of Denby Dale there emerged today an aroma of subtle fragrance. I can't tell you what
it will taste like. A security curtain has clamped down round the barn. But one of the cooks,
butcher Jack Hirst, emerged briefly with this progress report: 'Its rich . . . really rich.' Mr Hirst
smacked his lips with true Denby Dale appreciation of a pie. You can see the preparations in the
barn from a window high in one wall. Anticipatory hundreds queued today to jostle up the
gangplank leading to the platform outside the window. Through the mist inside they dimly
perceived Mr Hirst and his fellow cooks, attired in white aprons and with yellow gloves on their
hands, decanting buckets of rich-looking gravy into the mighty pie dish. The barn is barred to
intruders. 'Go away,' a cook shouted to photographers. Meanwhile flag-decked Denby Dale
braces itself for the day. Bunting is as thick as washing on a Monday. The accountant of the Pie
committee, Mr Keith Longbottom, is hoping that there will be no need to draw on the £7,500
insurance-against-rain policy.

Minutes before the pie was due to start its journey Jack Hirst raised a cheer from the hundreds
jostling outside the barn by announcing 'it's ready . . . and it's champion'.

Queues build at the barn at Dry Hill as people clamour to see the cooking process taking place. *(Huddersfield Examiner/Tolson Museum.)*

An hour later, and food and refreshments are available to the crowds who paid 1s to watch the cooks in action. *(Susan Buckley collection.)*

Jack Hirst, ready for duty in his role as head chef.

Jack Hirst (arms folded at the front) poses with his team in front of the oven prior to the great bake. Peter Holmes and Peter Fretwell are on the left. Joseph Kaye, Edward Hudson and Keith Harvey, far right, are also in the group. *(Susan Buckley collection.)*

Well into the cooking process. Pie guardian Raymond Haigh (white shirt, black trousers) gives a helping hand, just behind him is Jack Hirst, in the foreground wearing the gloves is Peter Fretwell. *(Susan Buckley collection.)*

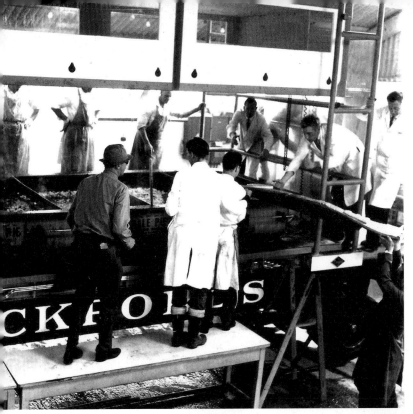

The meat and potato mixture can clearly be seen in the individual compartments of the pie dish as the chefs tend to their duties. *(Susan Buckley collection.)*

Raymond Haigh hands up more meat and potato to go into the pie, whilst Joseph Kaye uses a large mixing spoon stood on the gantry. *(Susan Buckley collection.)*

Chef, Joseph Kaye grabs a moment whilst the pie steams as it gently cooks. *(Susan Buckley collection.)*

Pieces of the huge pie crust, about to leave from Sheffield for Denby Dale.

Six pieces of the crust on the floor in the barn at Dry Hill. Each with two letters made of crust affixed to them spelling out the name 'Denby Dale'. *(Susan Buckley collection.)*

The relaxed faces say it all. The pie crust is on the dish and all is nearly ready. *(Susan Buckley collection.)*

127

The successful chefs who made the 1964 Denby Dale pie pose in the doorway of the cooking barn at Dry Hill. *(Susan Buckley collection.)*

The first moment of excitement for the hundreds of people waiting outside the barn came when the wooden screen blocking the entrance was moved aside. The crowd surged forward for their first glimpse of the giant. Minutes later the traction engine was reversed into the barn and the pie was carefully withdrawn.

At 2:00pm the pie left Hector Buckley's milking parlour under a striped canopy and was drawn by the *Marshall Foch*. As it arrived at the Dunkirk Inn the pie was given a tumultuous welcome. The men of the moment, the cooks, now held the place of honour immediately behind the pie, riding on a flat cart. Behind came a half-mile long procession of bands and floats, Miller Hill was safely negotiated and the parade made its way along High Street amidst the biggest crowds. The *Yorkshire Evening Post* noted that:

> *The pie, hidden under a cover with glass observation panels… was preceded by brass bands, pipe bands and military bands – seven in all – playing different tunes – but who cared? – and escorted by six West Riding policemen on prancing horses.*

128

The float of J Kitson & Sons waits at the junction of Dearneside and Miller Hill with its precious cargo, waiting to take its place in the pie procession. *(Susan Buckley collection.)*

The pie leaves the barn at Dry Hill.

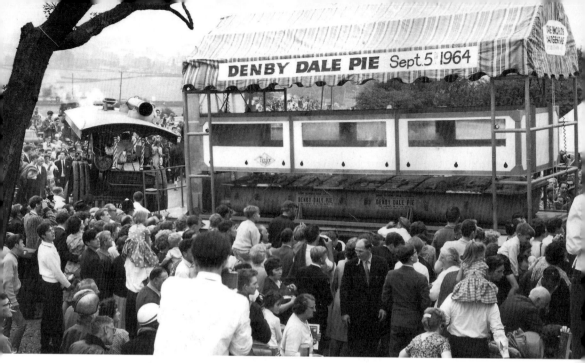

Crowds watch as the pie turns on to Dry Hill Lane to begin its journey around the village. *(Susan Buckley collection.)*

An aerial shot, showing the pie about to pass the Dunkirk Inn. *(Huddersfield Examiner/Tolson Museum.)*

The pie nears the end of Dry Hill, surrounded by well-wishers and photographers. *(Susan Buckley collection.)*

Now on Miller Hill the pie heads towards the cottages at Rombpickle.
(Susan Buckley collection.)

Crowds at Rombpickle, marquees and tents in the field behind include one for David Brown Tractors. The Zion Chapel can be seen on the skyline. *(Susan Buckley collection.)*

The pie safely negotiates Miller Hill.

An aerial photograph showing the newsagent's shop on the corner of Miller Hill with the corn mill buildings behind it. The crowds begin to line Wakefield Road. *(Huddersfield Examiner/Tolson Museum.)*

The crowds get bigger as the majestic *Marshal Foch* pulls the pie on Wakefield Road.

Souvenir programmes were available outside the newsagents and all around the village. *(Huddersfield Examiner/Tolson Museum.)*

An aerial photograph of the crowds waiting at the triangle near the White Hart. The pub itself can be seen to the left. *(Huddersfield Examiner/Tolson Museum.)*

Crowds in front of the White Hart await the pie. *(Susan Buckley collection.)*

The pie passes the cenotaph and gardens, today's village car park. The village Co-op can be seen behind.

The band began playing in the cenotaph car park at 10.00am and finished at around 6.00pm.
(*Huddersfield Examiner/Tolson Museum.*)

Stamina was required by the members of the band for their eight- hour session. Back row: left to right: Tommy Jackson, Gerard Paignton, Stewart Noble, Clifford Horsley. Front row: Ernest Fielder, Neil Tann, Alan Beever, Roy Wainwright.
(*Huddersfield Examiner/Tolson Museum.*)

Crowds await the pie on Wakefield Road, the houses on Wesley Terrace are behind them.
(Susan Buckley collection.)

Crowds waiting on High Street, towards the viaduct, the Prospect Inn is on the right.
(Susan Buckley collection.)

The great procession passes the assembled crowds on **High Street.** *(Susan Buckley collection.)*

A rear view of the pie, to the right is the yard belonging to Kitson's pipe manufacturers. *(Huddersfield Examiner/Tolson Museum.)*

Thousands watch and follow the pie amidst the flags and bunting on High Street.
(Huddersfield Examiner/Tolson museum.)

The cavalcade of floats, bands and other vehicles follows the pie up High Street, *(Susan Buckley collection.)*

139

The Barnsley Co-operative queen and attendant.

The pie queen vehicle is followed by the floral Barnsley Co-operative float. *(Huddersfield Examiner/Tolson Museum.)*

A closer view of the Barnsley Co-operative float.

Army vehicles, bands and more floats continue to pass the crowds on Wakefield Road.

Arthur Bellwood drives the tractor pulling the Cawthorne Young Farmers' Club float.

The National Savings
float following the
Kenyon's vehicle up
the High Street.

A closer view of the
National Savings float.
(Susan Buckley collection.)

142

The barrel shaped Whittaker's Ale's vehicle is followed by the Ringston's Tea car and the Mike Cox Mecca Band float. *(Susan Buckley collection.)*

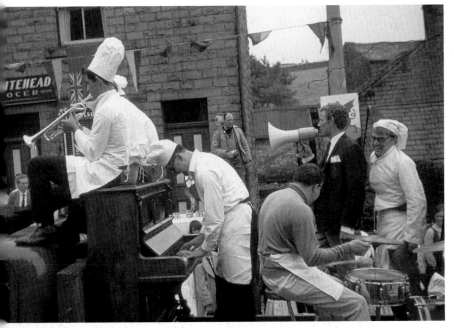

A closer view of the Mike Cox Mecca Band float.

The pie passes under the viaduct accompanied by large crowds.

Having watched the procession pass, thousands head down Norman Road, heading for the pie field in Norman Park.

An aerial view of Norman Park prior to the crowds arriving. The farm of Fred Bates is just off centre in front of the entertainment marquees. The pie serving platform is in the centre of the photograph with the village of Denby Dale in the background. *(Huddersfield Examiner/Tolson Museum.)*

As the fifteen-minute-long procession passed, the assembled crowds began to follow it, many taking a route down Norman Road, onto Hillside and then in to Norman Park. A slight hiccup occurred when the canopy of the trailer above the pie collided with overhead power cables, but these were quickly lifted to allow the pie access into its special enclosure in Norman Park.

Chairman John Hinchliffe welcomed everybody and then asked for silence while Denby Dale Brass Band played a hymn tune. The significance of the tune was in memory of the four victims of the fatal car accident at Grantham a week earlier, when one of the dead was a member of the band, Mr Lawrence Wainwright. Mr Wainwright's favourite hymn tune was Sandon *and the great crowd stood in silence and more than likely thought of the words of 'Lead, kindly light' to which hymn the tune is normally played.*

The Dalers put a brave face on for the day though all were mindful of the four men who were not there. The Denby Dale Band had started proceedings by playing *Abide With Me* at the War Memorial bandstand whilst respectful villagers stood to attention.

At 3.05pm, the pie was blessed by the Rector, Rev Geoffrey Lovejoy, and at 3.15pm Mr Jonas

The vast crowd gathers around the serving area in Norman Park, waiting for the arrival of the pie. *(Huddersfield Examiner/Tolson Museum.)*

The pie arrives, accompanied by the chefs and servers. *(Susan Buckley collection.)*

Probes still monitor the temperature of the pie, all is ready for the ceremonial opening. *(Huddersfield Examiner/Tolson Museum.)*

Kenyon performed the cutting ceremony. Jonas Kenyon, seventy-three-year-old former chairman of the Denby Dale UDC, was born and bred in the village. He was the son of William Henry Kenyon and grandson of the original Jonas Kenyon (1817-1890) who founded Dearneside Mills in Denby Dale in 1854. Mr Kenyon recalled being taken at the age of six to the 1896 pie by his father and he helped to collect money from various events in 1928. That year was something of a family affair as Mrs Kenyon led the team of cooks and Mr Kenyon's father-in-law, William Wood, opened the pie on that day.

In his speech, Jonas Kenyon said:

> *If as the result of today's effort we can build in Denby Dale a village hall as a centre of activities it will give the opportunity to regain and maintain a spirit of unity in the village, the same solid and independent spirit which animated this district a generation ago.*

He finished by declaring:

> *I declare this pie well and truly opened – it smells delicious.*

Jonas Kenyon prepares to cut the pie. To his left are chairman John Hinchliffe and the Rev Geoffrey Lovejoy. Immediately to his right is Frank Hobson. Head Chef Jack Hirst is to the extreme right of the photograph. *(Susan Buckley collection.)*

Peter Holmes, John Hinchliffe, Rev Lovejoy, Brian Kitson and Keith Harvey witness Mr Kenyon making history.

Peter Holmes, John Hinchliffe and Rev Lovejoy observe the first piece of crust being cut, Madge Greaves stands ready on the extreme right with a plate.

Madge Greaves comes to the rescue as the large piece of crust almost falls from the fork.

Peter Holmes and John Hinchliffe look a little worried, but the piece of pie is saved with a little intervention from Rev Lovejoy and Madge Greaves. Brian Kitson and Keith Harvey stand behind her. *(Susan Buckley collection.)*

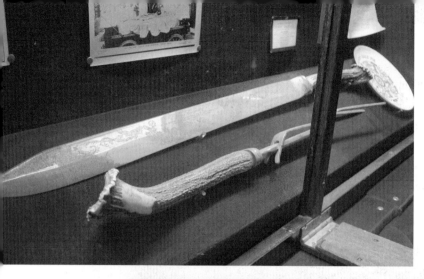

The ceremonial knife and fork used by Jonas Kenyon in 1964, now on display at Denby Dale Pie Hall.

Close up of the inscription to Jonas Kenyon on the ceremonial knife.

Serving begins, the former site of Inkerman Mill is to the left of centre on the skyline. Compare with the photograph taken in 1928. *(Huddersfield Examiner/Tolson Museum.)*

The multitude is reflected on the other side of the serving platform in Norman Park. *(Susan Buckley collection.)*

The individual crusts can clearly be seen next to the bowl of pie mixture as it is served. This lady was clearly over the moon with her portion.

(Susan Buckley collection.)

The small army of servers hard at work as the chefs fill up more plastic containers with pie. *(Susan Buckley collection.)*

Thousands of visitors wait for their portion of pie. *(Huddersfield Examiner/Tolson Museum.)*

Pie chairman, John Hinchliffe, lends a helping hand to the chefs, taking more pie and crust over to the servers.
(Susan Buckley collection.)

Alice Pell waits for head chef Jack Hirst and his colleagues to replenish her supply of pie to serve to the public.
(Susan Buckley collection.)

154

TV chef Phillip Harben looking suitably impressed with his portion of pie. *(Huddersfield Examiner/Tolson Museum.)*

Phillip Harben thought that the chances of the giant pie being better than the smaller ones he sampled would be a 'pious hope'. It has to be said, he looks more than satisfied on this photograph. *(Susan Buckley collection.)*

Pie publicity and press officer John Netherwood enjoying a slice of the monster pie that he helped to create. *(Huddersfield Examiner/ Tolson Museum.)*

Jonas Kenyon (centre) samples the pie that he officially opened, alongside the mayor and other dignitaries. *(Huddersfield Examiner/Tolson Museum.)*

By 3:20pm huge queues had formed as the pie was finally served to over 30,000 people, who were then entertained by the bands who had played in the procession, along with military marching and Morris Dancing. Bars, food and other refreshments were available all day alongside those offered by the village public houses. In the field behind the White Hart Inn, there was a wrestling show-ring featuring bouts including the famous Jim Breaks and The Royal Brothers. A concert put on by Huddersfield 'pop' manufacturer Ben Shaw was very well attended. An audience of around 600-700 listened to the music of the Thurlstone Hand Bell Ringers, Julie Wilde and to what was considered rather a surprise item, young Denby Dale pianist Robert Pell (twelve) who played four or five popular melodies accompanied by his father on the string bass.

The village bandstand was to be in use continuously for almost eight hours from 10:00am. Also behind the White Hart was a fairground and the venue for the grand finale of fireworks, which took place from 8:45pm. Up in Norman Park there were two more bandstands, the main refreshments bar, a large trade fair and of course the site for the arrival and distribution of the pie.

Although pie day was by no means hot and sunny, the rain held off until around 4:30pm, just as the last scrapings were being served from the dish. The rain did cause something of a stampede and many people left the village at this point. This was a pity as the rain did not last

Map showing the locations of the entertainment on offer during the day, originally featured inside the 1964 Souvenir Brochure.

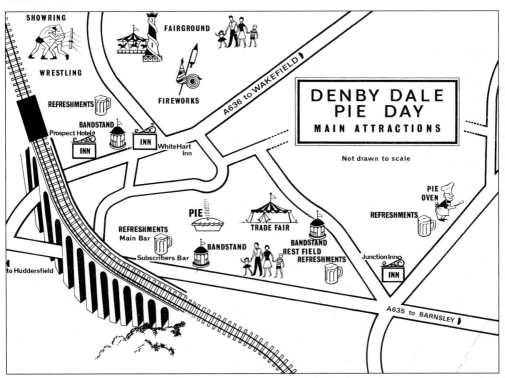

Crowds fill Norman Park to bursting, the pie can be seen to the right, almost on the skyline.

Morris Dancers entertain visitors near the fairground, the buildings of Naylor Brothers can be seen in the background.

A Scottish pipe marching band take over from the Morris Dancers. *(Susan Buckley collection.)*

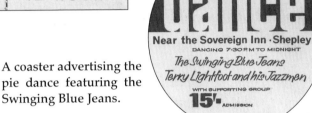

DENBY DALE PIE, 1964

Saturday, September 5th, 1964

Professional
Wrestling

12 NOON

n the Marquee on the Showground

6'-

TEAR OFF

DENBY DALE PIE
Sat., September 5th

Professional
Wrestling

6'-

12 NOON

An original ticket to the professional wrestling which began at noon on pie day.

Sat. September 5th.
GIANT DENBY DALE PIE

dance

Near the Sovereign Inn · Shepley
DANCING 7·30 P.M TO MIDNIGHT

The Swinging Blue Jeans
Terry Lightfoot and his Jazzmen
WITH SUPPORTING GROUP

15'- ADMISSION

A coaster advertising the pie dance featuring the Swinging Blue Jeans.

The fairground in full swing. To the left is a freak show booth, advertising such choice exhibits as 'the cat with six paws and the hen with four legs'. *(Susan Buckley collection.)*

TERRY LIGHTFOOT and his Jazzmen

A signed photograph of Terry Lightfoot and his Jazzmen obtained on the day by Madge Greaves, one of the pie servers.

At the Denby Dale Pie dance tonight

The Swinging Blue Jeans pose for a publicity still eating giant pieces of pie. The newspaper reported that a special clause in their contract allowed them to eat as much pie as they wanted.

long and the fairground and various sideshows suffered a little as a consequence. By 7:00pm, Denby Dale was likened to Piccadilly Circus as many more people arrived later to view the scene of the event and the police were still on point duty after 8:00pm.

A giant pie dance was also on offer near the Sovereign Inn, advertised in 'Pie News' – July 1964:

This promises to be a fab affair for the younger generation, music will come from the one and only Terry Lightfoot Band, plus one of the top groups in the country The Swinging Blue Jeans, supported by other groups.

The Swinging Blue Jeans were best known for their hits *Hippy Hippy Shake* (a number two hit in 1963) along with *Good Golly Miss Molly* and *You're No Good*.

According to the *Daily Mail*:

Six breweries fought for the concession to supply ale for the great day. Caterers, ice-cream manufacturers and fairground operators were locked in battle for Denby Dale's favour.

And so the party continued well into the night.

One week later and the committee could stand back and assess the success of the day.

DENBY DALE PIE   5th September, 1964

Summary of Income and Expenditure

	£	s	d	£	s	d	£	s	d
Efforts prior to Pie Day:									
Profit on—									
Bonfire and barbeque	102	8	7						
Christmas Cards	48	13	8						
Dances and Whist Drive	411	3	6						
Sing	25	11	6						
Car Rally	15	16	9						
Fashion Show	98	10	9						
Motor Cycle Scramble	156	7	3						
Traction Engine Rally	494	11	8						
Film Show	35	4	2						
Denby Players	14	9	9						
Coffee Mornings	85	1	3						
Harvest Festival	15	15	0	1503	13	10			
Less Loss on—									
Gala	124	11	4						
Raffles	45	10	0	170	1	4			
Net Profit on efforts prior to Pie Day							1333	12	6
Pie Day Income									
Sales of Brochures and Souvenirs	14952	8	7						
Other Income—Pie Dish viewing, Wrestling and selling rights etc.	2269	14	6	17222	3	1			
Less—									
Cost of Souvenirs	4790	6	0						
Cost of Pie	1215	19	5	6006	5	5			
							11215	17	8
Subscriptions	455	16	0						
Profit on Dance	234	2	5						
Car Park Fees (net)	394	14	6						
Bank Interest	264	9	0	1349	1	11			
							12564	19	7
Less Expenses—									
Cost of Tents, Scaffolding, Sound Equipment, etc	1591	2	2						
Cost of Bands, Prizes and Decorations	680	7	5						
Insurance	937	5	0						
Public Relations and Food Fair	2223	19	4						
General Expenses—Printing, Advertising, Legal, etc.	1900	10	2	7333	4	1			
Net Profit on Pie Day							5231	15	6
Total Profit on Denby Dale Pie 1964							£6565	8	0

NOTE: There may be a tax liability of £109

Balance sheet showing the financial results of the 1964 pie.

Cigarette manufacturers John Player & Sons donated a trophy for the best decorated pie float, which went to the winners Jonas Kenyon & Sons. William Kenyon accepted the trophy on behalf of the company from G E Doughty, representative of John Player. The float was decorated by employees of the firm under the direction of Norman Firth and menders rode on the float in the procession. The float featured past Denby Dale pies. Back row, left to right: ?, Christine Town, ?, Sybil Turner, Ann Sowerby. Front row, left to right: Margaret Blacker, ?, ?, Christine Hitchins, W E Doughty, William Kenyon, Sheila Wainwright, ?, Delia Smith, ?, Margaret Saville, Norman Firth, ?, Rita Lockwood.

Huddersfield Examiner:

Pie Men Tot Up Their Profit (week after the pie).
Publicity manager John Netherwood said, 'one thing is certain, we've raised at least enough to build a village community centre'. Mr Fred Thorpe, a local bank manger totted up the proceeds from the sale of 30,000 portions of pie at 2s 6d, the 20,000 souvenir plates which sold for 7s 6d apiece, the 10,000 mugs and tankards sold at between 3s and 17s 6d and thousands of 2s 6d brochures. The only hitch on the day was the rain, which drove thousands of people away, though this did not arrive until 4:30pm. The pie dish, covered by an imitation piecrust made of plaster of paris and wire mesh, was driven on a lorry to London where it was exhibited at the Food Fair at Olympia. Packed inside the dish were 5,000 brochures, 2,000 souvenir plates and 1,000 small replica meat and potato pies made to the same recipe as the giant, which are to be sold at Olympia to swell the pie fund profits.

The pie float created by the staff of Jonas Kenyon & Sons.

'Pie Madness' reported in the local newspaper. The pie dish did not, in fact, ever make this difficult journey.

Huddersfield Weekly Examiner

SATURDAY, SEPTEMBER 5, 1964

DENBY DALE PIE SOUVENIR

1788 and all that

1788 Commemorating recovery of King George III. from mental illness.

1815 Commemorating Battle of Waterloo.

1846 Commemorating Repeal of the Corn Laws.

1887 Commemorating Queen...

After Capt. Webb, Bleriot and the hovercraft...

CHANNEL BID BY THE PIE-DISH?

DENBY DALE'S great pie dish, the only floating pie dish in the world, may soon be blazing a new trail of adventure. For there's talk of a cross-Channel enterprise in the wake of today's big Pie Day occasion.

What may seem, on the face of things, to be just another fantastic whim is, "The Examiner" understands, being considered in all seriousness. Pie publicity chairman John Netherwood assured us he wasn't joking when he said, "We believe it would be a formidable technical challenge to sail the dish across the Channel. But, like a pie to feed 30,000 people, it could be achieved."

The plan—which the Pie Committee propose to hammer out after Pie Day is over—is for the dish to sail from Dover to the French coast.

It would be powered by two outboard motors, as was the case earlier this year when the dish had its...

From abroad for the Pie

He will wield the big knife

MR. JONAS KENYON, a seventy-three-year-old former chairman of Denby Dale Urban District Council, is the man who will wield the 3ft-long knife and fork which have been specially made for the...

What's on in Denby Dale

10-00 Trade Fair Opens. Show Ring programme begins at Show Field in Cumberworth Lane.

12-00 Wrestling in marquee at Show Field.

2-00 Pie procession leaves Dry Hill Farm.

2-50 Pie arrives at Norman Park.

3-15 Pie cutting by Mr. Jonas Kenyon.

3-25 Distribution of 30,000 portions begins.

6-00 (onwards) Concert, Dancing, Fireworks, etc.

(For fuller details see...

A poignant and permanent reminder of the sacrifice made by one of the beasts slaughtered to provide meat for the 1964 pie. The horns are now on display at the Pie Hall in the village.

This was not quite the end for the Pie Committee. Some time soon after the death of Winston Churchill (24 January 1965) they were involved in a football match against determined local opposition:

> A team from the Denby Dale Pie Committee played a team from the George Inn, Upper Denby. After a minute's silence in memory of Sir Winston Churchill, the George team got off to a fine start and were 3–1 in the lead when coffee and rum was served at half time. Eventually the George Inn team won 5–4, goals being scored for the winners by P Bower (2), K S Longbottom (2) and R Wydell; the scorers for the Pie Committee being K Harvey (2), J Netherwood and J Bott. The pie goal was under pressure for most of the match and the score was only kept to 5 by the brilliance of goalkeeper M Kitson and full backs Raymond Haigh and John Hinchliffe.

The Pie Committee met for the final time and was wound up in September 1965 in the canteen of Z Hinchliffe & Sons.

Chapter 10

1972

Denby Dale Pie Hall

In 1964 a Trust Deed had been drawn up, the object of which was to use the funds generated through pie day to acquire land for a village hall to be built upon in Denby Dale. The trustees of the charity were John N Hinchliffe (chairman), George H Naylor, John Haigh and Alice Pell. As we have noted, John Haigh was killed in the traffic accident on the way back from filming in London and his place was taken by John Netherwood. The final amount raised on pie day was £6,573, and by 1969, this sum had increased due to good investment to nearly £10,000. A grant of £10,000 made by the Department of Education and Science through the Yorkshire Rural Communities Council increased the amount of funds available.

A newspaper report dated 13 March 1968 appeared under the headline:

BBC Newsman Probes Denby Dale Pie Fund Dispute

BBC Yorkshire *Look North* cameras came to the village to investigate what was happening to the proceeds of the 1964 pie. Reporter John Burns, spoke to Norah Kitson Smith who was unhappy about the length of time that had elapsed since 1964 and that nothing had been done. She claimed that she had offered the committee a plot of land of about 600 square yards near Denby Dale church but that this had been rejected as being an unsuitable site. Clr John Netherwood (and former publicity officer for the 1964 pie), explained that since 1964, twenty one meetings had been held in order to try and find a suitable site to provide a hall deserving of the village. He said that the committee were interested in buying the Centenary Memorial Hall and had made an offer of £5,500 that the trustees were prepared to accept. Unfortunately, the Methodist owners of the premises had insisted that there should be no alcoholic drinks or gaming on the premises and this was proving a stumbling block. The idea was to develop the building so that it could be used for dances, socials, wedding receptions, bingo, indeed anything that the villagers may require. The restriction imposed by the Methodists meant that the proposed grant from the Yorkshire Rural Communities Council would be adversely affected. The Methodist

THE PIE HALL
at
DENBY DALE

A registered charity devoted to the service and leisure diversions of the people of Denby Dale and their friends.

Brochure for the Pie Hall.

Denby
Dale
Pie
Hall

Opening, 5th September, 1972

Cutting the Pie, 5th September, 1964

Brochure for the opening of the Pie Hall.

Inside the brochure, details included the Trustees and Management Committee.

FOREWORD

by Reginald Beever Esq.
Chairman Pie Hall Management Committee

I am greatly honoured to be associated with this delightful building which is the proud achievement of the 1964 Denby Dale Pie effort.

I wish to express my sincere appreciation to all those whose untiring efforts over the past eight years has made possible the provision of a permanent village hall from which all members of the local community can derive great pleasure and benefit.

The future management of the hall is now in the hands of a very efficient and enthusiastic committee whose efforts so far should ensure the success of this great venture.

TRUSTEES

Mrs. A. Pell.   Mr. J. N. Hinchliffe.   Mr. G. Naylor.

MANAGEMENT COMMITTEE

Chairman: Treasurer: Secretary:
R. Beever.   K. S. Longbottom.   M. R. A. Hollingworth

Jane Beevers, Shirley Firth, Jim W. Buckley, Hector Buckley, William W. Kenyon, Brian Kitson, W. John Netherwood, Joe R. W. Price, Stanley Schofield, Richard White.

In addition to the hundred or more people who have worked and given of their time and money.

Donations are gratefully received from

A. W. Bain Ltd
R. Beever
R. K. Beever Esq., J.P.
Mr. & Mrs. A. J. Bennett
Mr. & Mrs. J. C. Bennett
Denby Dale & District Play Group
Denby Dale Ladies Circle
Mr. & Mrs. M. Fletcher
Hirst Buckley Ltd
Peter Holmes
C. Kavazi
Mr. Jonas Kenyon
Jonas Kenyon & Sons Ltd
Mr. C. Lazenby
Mr. & Mrs. C. R. Marsden
Naylor Bros. (Denby Dale) Ltd
Netherwood Dalton & Co. Ltd
Phoenox Textiles Ltd
A. H. S. Waters & Partners
Mr. & Mrs. G. Walsh
Welconstruct Company Ltd
West Riding Shirt Company Ltd
Executors Herbert Wilcox

PROGRAMME

Tuesday 5th September

OPENING CEREMONY by Councillor Jonas Kenyon.
Denby Dale Pie and Pea Supper.

7.30 p.m.   Admission FREE

Wednesday 6th September

CONCERT
Thurlstone Bell Ringers
Conductor: A. Dyson.

Denby Dale Ladies Choir
Conductor : Mrs. A. Jones.
Pianist: J. Kenyon.

Denby Dale Band
Conductor: Richard Horn.

7.30 p.m.   Admission 15 p.
               O.A.P.'s   7 p.

Thursday 7th September

OPEN NIGHT

Art Exhibition
History of the Pies Exhibition
Flower Arrangement Exhibition by Mrs. Y. Stephenson
Film of the 1964 Pie by Huddersfield Cine Club

Refreshments available.

7.30 - 10 p.m. Admission FREE

Friday 8th September

GALA SUPPER DANCE

Dancing to Gilbert Pell Quintet.

With Artistes Margaret Whitwam.
          Piano: Derek Walton.
                    Bobby Ray & Kieran Lane.

8 p.m. - 2 a.m. Admission £1. 50 to include supper.

Saturday 9th September

FOLK NIGHT

With the 7 Folk

Merry Taylor

Mag. Vere and Robert

7.45 p.m.   Admission 15 p.

Minister at Denby Dale, Rev J W Chapman, was not optimistic of the transaction going through. He had initially approached the committee with the idea as the building was underused and was becoming a burden to maintain, £1,600 had recently been spent on repairs to the roof. Ultimately the restrictions were unacceptable, the Methodist Trustees refused to back down and the idea came to nothing, the building was later demolished in 1977.

In late 1969 Birkwood House in the centre of Denby Dale and a piece of land adjoining it were purchased by the Trustees for £2,100, and it was converted into the desired village hall for £23,847.00. It was opened on 5 September 1972, exactly eight years after the pie day itself.

Outside the building, Reginald Beever, chairman of the Management Committee, invited Clr Jonas Kenyon to perform the opening ceremony. Clr Kenyon said:

I would like to say how pleased I was to receive your invitation to open the Pie Hall. It is eight years ago today, when on 5 September 1964 I had the honour to open the largest of all the Denby Dale pies. This was the culmination of two years of hard work and activity by the members of Denby Dale and district and was supported by our friends near and far. It has been said it is almost as difficult to spend money, specially public money, as to make it, but I believe the right decision was made in trying to find a central site in the village before deciding where to build. I hope there will be another pie. It has been said that the same generation makes one pie and only one. I think they know what work it involves. However, from today it is just about

Julie White presents a bouquet to Mary Hollingworth at the opening of the Pie Hall. Looking on from left to right are Mrs F Beever, Reginald Beever (chairman of the Pie Hall Management Committee) and Jonas Kenyon.

the right period of time for another generation to tackle another pie (larger of course) to celebrate the advent of the year 2000. I think that the people of Denby Dale will not let the event pass without notice and I wish them the best of luck, I would say for the future: Carry on Denby Dale, carry on.

One of the 300 guests who attended the official opening ceremony was Bill Venables, the previous owner of Birkwood House. Now living in Huddersfield, he thought that a really good job had been done:

Relatives on my mother's side built the house and I am very pleased indeed at the way it's turned out.

Inside a plaque was erected on the wall in memory of the four committee members killed in the fateful car crash only days before the event in 1964. Today the hall is used by such groups as the Women's Institute, Darby & Joan Club, The Amateur Radio Club, Flower Club, Keep Fit Classes and Old Time Dancing. None of the groups pay a hire fee but give the Pie Hall a donation each year in accordance with their available resources.

There was now a place, not only to commemorate the village's pie making traditions but also a site to display the most recent dish:

Huddersfield Examiner 1975:

Pie dish will take its place in history

The Denby Dale pie dish, which brought fame to the tiny West Yorkshire village eleven years ago, is to be 'rescued' and given a new lease of life. Officials are to remove it from the pipe manufacturing works where it is gathering rubbish and corrosion, clean it and polish it and erect it on a plinth of glory outside the Denby Dale Pie Hall. The restored dish will be ceremonially unveiled by Mr Richard Wainwright, Liberal MP for Colne Valley on 6 September at the end of eight days of nostalgic celebrations. 'We thought it would have been almost criminal to have left the dish to rot away unremembered,' said Mr John Netherwood, publicity officer to the original pie committee. The sorry plight of the once-proud pie dish was highlighted in the Yorkshire Post on 9 September, last year when it was revealed that it was being used to test corrosion at the works of the Cawthorne firm making vitrified clay sewer pipes. At that time officials gave an undertaking that the pie dish would be rescued and restored and this, said Mr John Netherwood, was what was now being done. The dish has had a chequered career. Launched on a river it quickly sank, but was salvaged for the big day. Later it was exhibited at Olympia and there were plans, never fulfilled, for it to be sailed across the Channel. Its resurrection and role of honour will be proceeded by other events, such as exhibitions, film shows of the 1964 bake, races, a cricket match and the manning of a special 'ham' radio station with the call sign DDP.

The 1964 pie dish remains at the Pie Hall to this day; it takes pride of place at the front of the building acting as a raised flowerbed.

The Pie Hall with the 1964 pie dish in front.

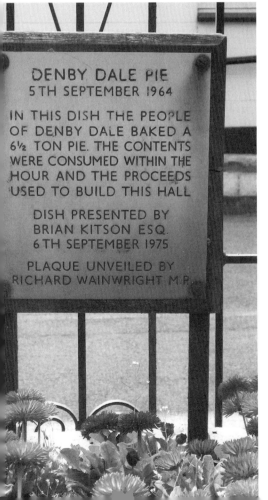

DENBY DALE PIE
5TH SEPTEMBER 1964

IN THIS DISH THE PEOPLE
OF DENBY DALE BAKED A
6½ TON PIE. THE CONTENTS
WERE CONSUMED WITHIN THE
HOUR AND THE PROCEEDS
USED TO BUILD THIS HALL

DISH PRESENTED BY
BRIAN KITSON ESQ.
6TH SEPTEMBER 1975

PLAQUE UNVEILED BY
RICHARD WAINWRIGHT M.P.

The 1964 pie dish, now a huge flowerbed, spring 2011.

Plaque above the 1964 pie dish.

Chapter 11

3 September 1988

The Bicentenary Pie

Pie No. 9

The village of Denby Dale had seen many changes since the first recorded pie festivities in 1788. Most notably was the growth and subsequently rapid demise of its industry. By 1988 only one of the three large textile manufacturers was left, Jonas Kenyon's, and the Brownhill's Group had ceased trading leaving only Z Hinchliffe & Sons as a mass employer in the village. The corn mill at the bottom of Miller Hill was demolished by 1975 and replaced with new housing, the estate now being called Brookside. In 1976 the old school on Wakefield Road had closed and moved to a new site at the top of the Gilthwaites estate and the village, as a whole, had become more of a residential area playing its part in the commuter age.

The traditional close-knit ties within the village community had all but evaporated but towards the end of 1985 a number of meetings occurred with a view to turning back the clock and celebrating the village's famous traditions in the only style possible. A new Pie Committee was formed which decided that celebrations should be held in 1988 to commemorate 200 years of pie making in the village. A monster pie to celebrate baking monster pies.

The Executive Committee members were:
Chairman – Graham Fussey (an occupational therapist with the Barnsley Health Authority). Ann Ashworth, Susan Horne, John Cook, Ann Littlewood, Mike Elliott, Marcus Kitson, Howard Jackson, Dennis Tremble, Phillip Robinson, Ray Fowler, Brian Woodhead, Sheila Fewster, Barrie Clarke, Celia Somerville, Stan Ward, Janet Hepworth, Gerald Moffatt (vice chairman), Ahmed Pochee and Wyn Outram.

To generate funds for expenses incurred along the way fundraising events were organised. These included a Halloween dance and a cheese and wine luncheon and 200 people attended

Graham Fussey, chairman of the Pie '88 Committee.

a barbecue. These were followed in 1987 when a human horse race night took place and a fashion show attracted more than 400 people.

The venture achieved charitable status and officially launched the baking of a pie on the 18 March 1987, the date for the big day being 3 September 1988. The committee decided that the celebrations should continue on into the Sunday, a two-day festival to commemorate 200 years.

The committee wasted no time in swinging into action. Pie memorabilia was commissioned, including launch night plates as well as the usual well-established plates. The design of the traditional plate was chosen by competition and was won by Mr J Pearson of Penistone. These plates retailed at £8.50. A further, limited edition plate was also produced, this by Peter Jones China and Glassware of Wakefield. Limited to 2,000 plates, these retailed at £40.

A touring caravan, known as the Denby Dale Pie Roadshow, travelled far and wide promoting the big day, a float was prepared for the Denby Dale Carnival 1987 and a Post Office box number was acquired to allow the public to write for up to date information.

It was also in 1987 that Billington Structures of Wombwell, Barnsley agreed to build and sponsor the pie dish. Made of mild steel it measured 20 feet by 7 feet by 1½ feet deep and weighed around half a ton, and was designed to hold 7 cubic metres of pie. The souvenir programme of the day's events gave the recipe in full:

2800 or 3000kg – prime English beef.
2800 or 3000kg – potatoes
700kg – onions

700kg – gravy and specially prepared seasoning
75sq metres – glazed puff pastry – cut into 10cm squares
1,500kg – flour
1,200kg – margarine
salt – a big pinch

utensils:

forty – 100 gramme ladles
eighty – food carrying receptacles (bucket shaped)
50,000 – pre printed serving dishes
50,000 – sponsored serviettes
50,000 – forks and spoons
180 – sets of caterers uniforms (including hair nets)
eighty – stacking plastic trays (each to hold fifty-six portions of pastry)
one – steel dish – measuring 6.5m x 2.25m x 0.55m
one – travelling oven
two – steam generators
two – hot water generators
one – large open plan building

The pie was to be the biggest ever and it was hoped to be able to serve 50,000 people, but since 1964 a lot of the rules had changed, as had the methods of cooking. Consideration had to be given to everything including suitable ingredients and utensils, and parading and serving the pie in order to comply Environmental Health requirements. Luckily members of that government department were very supportive. The floor of the barn at Broomfield House, Upper Denby, where the pie was to be cooked was lined with polythene and was specially treated to make sure that no dust could rise. The cooking was done as follows:

From the Souvenir Pie 1988 Brochure:

The process consists of the meat filling being cooked in steam kettles in ¼ tonne batches, and filled into twelve trays contained with one big tray. Circulating hot water around and within the small trays will maintain the required temperature. Heat losses are controlled by suitable insulation. The parading of the ppie will take approximately an hour, after which it will be connected to another hot water generator to maintain the contents at serving temperature. During the parade the residual heat and the insulation will ensure that the temperature does not fall below the critical level. During the parade a levelling system utilising air-jacks will be used to overcome the gradients along the route.

Ahmed Pochee, a laboratory manager for Lyons Bakery of Barnsley, was the chairman of The Pie Trusts Technical Committee and was in charge of these activities. Howard Gamble, also of Lyons Bakery was in charge of the team of twelve cooks (mainly members of the Pie Committee).

Prior to the day and as with 1964, a trial baking was organised by Mr Pochee at the Travellers

Rest pub. This was attended by, amongst others, the directors of Hildale Dairies, Scissett who were instrumental in organising the purchase of the ingredients of the pie and made a sizeable donation towards the cost. Stephen Brook (chairman), Tony Hinchliffe, Hector Buckley, Phillip Holmes, Brian Buckley and Peter Jebson tasted this sample of the big day and Hector Buckley kept up his association with the pies of Denby Dale.

One of the more pleasant aspects of promoting the pie, was the competition to choose the bicentenary pie queen. The judges comprised: Graham Fussey chairman of the Pie Committee, Eileen Hepworth (wife of Denby Dale butcher Keith), Bronwyn Hill (of Bronwyn's Fashions, Denby Dale), Peter Holmes (butcher, Denby Dale & Penistone) and Patrick Brooke (chief reporter of the *Huddersfield District Chronicle*). They chose Janet Armitage, sixteen (daughter of Mr & Mrs Ken Armitage of Withyside, Denby Dale) as the winner, who received £150 clothes voucher and a holiday in Spain. The runner up was Julie Peace aged sixteen. Joint third were Joanne Somerville, sixteen, Suzanne Maskell, seventeen and Lisa Cook, eighteen.

The winner of the competition and 1988 pie queen – Janet Armitage.

The five contestants in the 1988 Pie queen competition, left to right: Lisa Cook, Suzanne Maskell, Julie Peace, Joanne Somerville and Janet Armitage.

It was also necessary to consider the traffic and parking problems, which would undoubtedly arise on the day. The committee placed great emphasis on the use of public transport, a Pie Rover Metro ticket was produced for the day and bus and rail timetables were adjusted and altered so that the services would pass the pie field. Local farmers donated their land to provide car parking to facilitate a park-and-ride operation subsidised by the Pie Trust. Also consulted were the police, Environmental Health, the St John's Ambulance and West Yorkshire Ambulance Services. Massive crowds were expected to attend the first two-day Denby Dale pie. A circular was produced by West Yorkshire Police asking all local residents for co-operation in keeping roads clear and informing them of restrictions. In all the event was policed by 100 full and part time officers aided by special constables and one helicopter.

Advertising leaflet for the 1988 pie.

In early 1988 scholars at Scissett Middle School planted potatoes and onions, which, when harvested, were to be used in the pie. Publicity culminated in both radio and television coverage. Martin Wiley narrated *The Big Pie* on Radio Leeds, which included interviews with some of the 1988 trustee's along with Raymond Haigh, David Bostwick and old Daler, the late Joseph Peace. The BBC also made a half hour television documentary, narrated by Harry Gration it presented a brief history of the pies and culminated with footage taken during the proceedings of the 1988 event. The programme was broadcast the following week.

During the week before the big day, heavy rain had waterlogged the pie field site on Barnsley Road and had left the organisers with a few headaches. Press officer Barrie Clarke admitted that on the Friday:

> *The outlook had seemed bleak, and it had not done much for our enthusiasm when a television presenter who visited the field on Friday night described the site as a washed-out, windswept spot.*

As tents and marquees began to go up, interest and anticipation increased. The funfair arrived and little-by-little the rain-sodden mud baths, which had been fields, gradually yielded to the tractors hauling in the lorries and equipment. Hopes grew when the weather forecast for the weekend held an improvement. This first two-day extravaganza desperately needed good weather to succeed.

Events planned for Saturday, aside from the pie were pipe bands, an escapologist, a parachute drop and a Chinese lion dance. Children were catered for with a bouncy castle, a baby elephant and Pickles the Clown. Radio Leeds would be making regular broadcasts from the pie field and in other areas were steam engines, a hot air balloon, army bikes and a helicopter pad (for flights over the pie field). The day was due to finish with a fireworks display. Sunday was almost as good, besides a donkey derby, another parachute drop, Morris Dancers and an RSPCA dog show, the BBC Radio One Roadshow and its host, Mike Read, were going to be broadcasting live to the nation from the pie field.

An awful lot hinged on the weather . . . on Saturday morning the sun was shining, and the Gods were on the side of the Pie 88 Trust.

The pie left its oven at Upper Denby a little after midday. Cooking had gone well and a small crowd witnessed the lorry belonging to R J Tait & Son haul the monster pie, covered by a blue-and-white canopy into Bank Lane. It moved on into Denby Lane and down the hill towards the Dunkirk public house where crowds of people were waiting, being entertained by Hade Edge Band. The trailer carrying the pie had sixteen wheels to enable it to carry its load of more than 7 tons, driven by Susan Ross it made its way down into the decorated village, safely negotiating Miller Hill and then turned left into Wakefield Road where the crowds were thickest. Joining it were the members of a massive, mile-long procession, which included the *Marshal Foch* of 1964 pie fame, scouts, Morris Dancers, floats, brass bands, a Scottish bagpipes band and people in fancy dress.

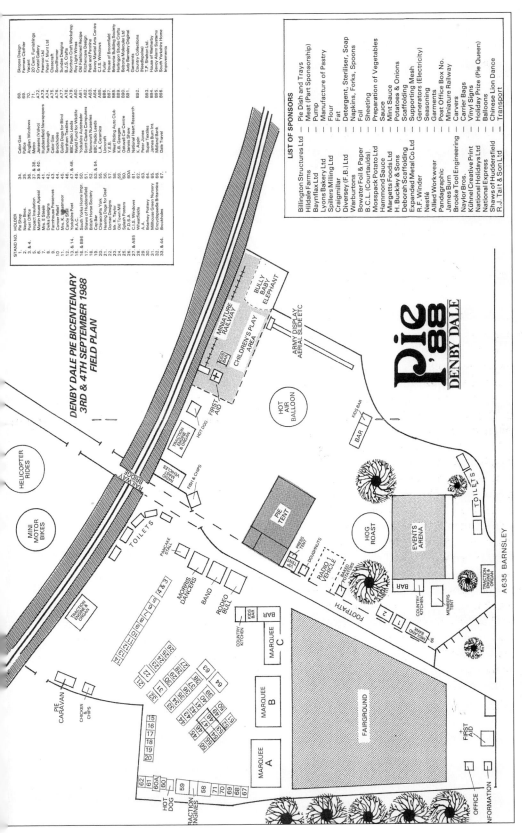

Plan of the 1988 pie field.

A first glimpse of the pie as it leaves the barn at Broomfield House, where it was cooked, and turns on to Bank Lane in Upper Denby.

After negotiating the narrow twisting road the pie moves down Smithy Hill, Upper Denby heading for Lower Denby.

The crowds welcome the pie at Lower Denby. *(Susan Buckley collection.)*

A busy scene where the pie had to weave its way through thousands of well-wishers and tourist busses at the Dunkirk. Once through here it made its way down Miller Hill, where it joined the rest of the huge procession. *(Susan Buckley collection.)*

Now on Wakefield Road, the procession has begun in earnest. Field Co-ordinator and transport and security organiser John Cook oversees matters on his radio.

As the pie travels past the golden brown crust can easily be seen. Unfortunately, all of this was thrown away because of health and safety reasons.

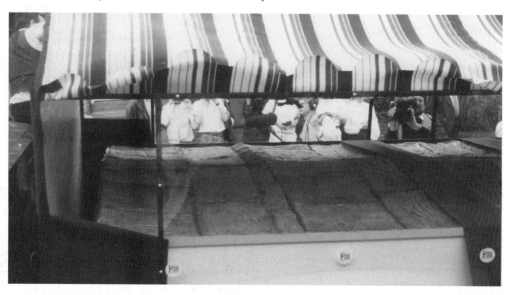

The pie heads towards the viaduct followed by the long procession.

1988 pie queen Janet Armitage travelled in style.

The Round Table float.

The Shire horses of builder D Parker.

Molly, the traction engine owned by John Slater, his son Steven is seated in front of the back wheel.

Traditional dance and brass bands also took part in the procession.

The Pie Hall float.

A jazz band livened up the crowds whenever they passed.

The pie on Barnsley Road (K-Line) on the final stage of its journey.

Pie queen Janet Armitage waves to the crowds on Barnsley Road. *(Susan Buckley collection.)*

A traditional photograph as the pie passes under the skew arch of the viaduct. *(Susan Buckley collection.)*

5 September - *Huddersfield Examiner:*

The sun shone, the crowds came, the bands played and the pie was hot and tasty. Excitement mounted as [Hade Edge] Band marched out into the road to take its place in front of the pie. The golden brown crust was clearly visible through the perspex panels on the side of the sixteen-wheeled trailer. There was a moment of drama as the cab and trailer came to a halt, then rolled back an inch or two as it was taking the awkward uphill turn into the main road. It was three or four long minutes before the manoeuvre was successfully completed. Susan Ross, thirty-five, driving the cab for R J Tait and Son, explained later that some of the wheels on the four back axles had left the ground because of the angle of the corner.

The rest of the parade passed without incident as the pie reached its final destination. Two tractors helped its entry into the muddy, hard-core covered conditions of the pie field and painfully slowly it reached its destination.

Eager crowds watch the vehicle's sticky progress through the mud. *(Susan Buckley collection.)*

The pie enters the muddy field off Barnsley Road. *(Susan Buckley collection.)*

A tractor is employed to help the pie negotiate the muddy final stretch of its journey. *(Susan Buckley collection.)*

Finally, the pie halts under the cutting and serving marquee. *(Susan Buckley collection.)*

The striped canopy above the pie is removed as the invited dignitaries begin to assemble.

Almost ready. John Hinchliffe, to the front left, looks upon the creation. Chairman Graham Fussey can be seen discussing some last minute details with press officer Barrie Clarke. On the stage behind the pie are John Cook, chairman of the Technical Committee Ahmed Pochee and chef Howard Gamble. *(Susan Buckley collection.)*

Thousands queue on the Barnsley Road eager to get into the pie field. *(Susan Buckley collection.)*

More queuing, this time awaiting distribution of the pie. *(Susan Buckley collection.)*

5 September - *Huddersfield Examiner:*

After the perspex panels and awning had been removed the Mayor of Kirklees, Clr John Holt led three cheers for the pie. Grace was said by the Bishop of Pontefract, the Rt Rev Richard Hare and Pie Committee chairman, Graham Fussey, presented specially made 2 foot long servers to local businessman Mr John Hinchliffe, who cut the first piece of pie. He thanked the committee for their efforts, saying that a lot of hard work, as well as meat and potatoes, had gone into the pie-making.

A bank of newspaper photographers jostle for the best position to see John Hinchliffe make the ceremonial first cut into the pie. *(Susan Buckley collection.)*

The first cut. With a flourish John Hinchliffe opens the pie, to his left is Ann Taylor MP, behind him pie chairman Graham Fussey and to his right the Mayor of Kirklees Clr John Holt and the Mayoress Pamela Baguley. *(Above: Susan Buckley collection, below: Huddersfield Examiner.)*

The ceremonial knife and fork, now on display at the Pie Hall.

The team of 170 servers were quickly in business, people paid £1 for a 4oz portion of pie with crust on a decorated polystyrene plate with plastic utensils. Faye Mannion, at that time a pupil at Scissett Middle School, created the design on the polystyrene plate. The pie was deemed to be good. Indeed local MP, Ann Taylor (formerly Leader of the House), described the pie as *absolutely delicious*. It was over two hours before the lengthy queues began to subside. The two-feet long silver carvers used by John Hinchliffe were hand-made by Vincent Mulcrone in Sheffield, through sponsorship by Brooke Tool Engineering Holdings.

The cooks now begin to serve the pie. *(Susan Buckley collection.)*

An army of servers begins to feed the assembled thousands. *(Susan Buckley collection.)*

Servers, surrounded by boxes of plastic knives and forks, polystyrene trays and pieces of crust. *(Susan Buckley collection.)*

And still the crowds queue, well over an hour after serving began. *(Susan Buckley collection.)*

The eighth compartment is now open as crowds continue to surround the pie.

The servers continue operations inside the pie marquee. *(Susan Buckley collection.)*

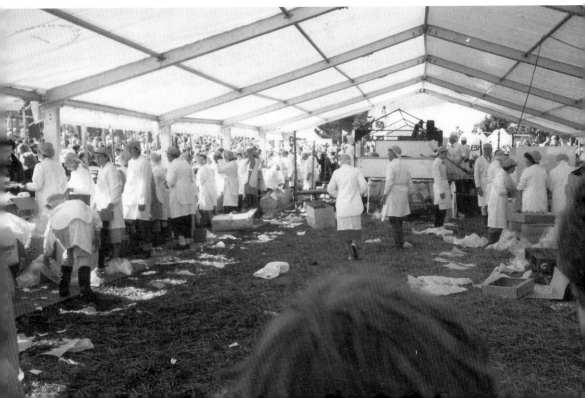

Dishing up yet another portion of the pie. *(Susan Buckley collection.)*

Pie queen Janet Armitage enjoys her portion of pie. To the left is Clr John Holt, Mayor of Kirklees and to the right is pie queen attendant Lisa Cook. *(Susan Buckley collection.)*

Some of the servers pause for a moment for a group photograph as a memento of their special day. *(Susan Buckley collection.)*

Police placed the attendance figure at around 100,000 people.

The Mayor and Mayoress of Kirklees, John Holt and Pamela Baguley, sample the pie. *(Susan Buckley collection.)*

The last of the crust has been removed as stocks of the pie begin to dwindle.

Serving continued for over two hours. *(Susan Buckley collection.)*

Pie queen Janet Armitage and attendant Lisa Cook pose with an exhibitor. *(Susan Buckley collection.)*

Clr Philip Naylor paid tribute to the members of the Pie Committee, he said:

They must have suffered many anxious moments, not least of all during the atrocious weather conditions of mid-week. The end product was absolutely marvellous. I was overcome by the whole spirit of the occasion and felt very proud to be there.

Despite all the hard work by the Trust, there were many problems on the day. Traffic congestion resulted in long waits for the advertised free park-and-ride services, both arriving and leaving the pie field. Many people gatecrashed the festivities as the only entrance to the arena was swamped with people, and walls were broken down as they swept into the field free of charge prompting the police and marshals to guard certain sections of the ground. Despite all this there were no arrests and no major incidents. Police figures placed the crowd number at 100,000 on the day (though this was likely to have been nearer 60,000). This was followed up on Sunday with a further 30,000 who attended the Radio One Roadshow, which began at 11:00am and was broadcast live from 1:00pm till 3:00pm:

Large numbers stood in the sunshine enjoying the Radio One Roadshow. Top disc jockey, Mike Read took part in some zany antics as he played request records for crowd members and led a sixties disco quiz during a two-hour live broadcast.

Mike Read on the Radio One Roadshow vehicle.

Mike Read broadcasting live from the pic
field, alongside Postman Pat.

Mike Read with
a member of the
audience taking
part in a
competition.

Large crowds attended the first pie Sunday.

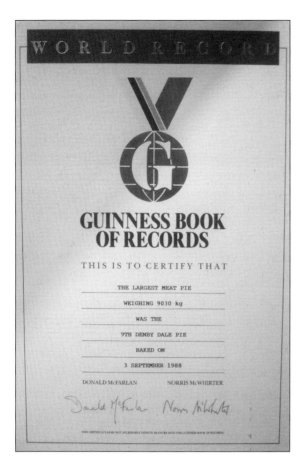

The certificate presented to the Pie 1988 Committee by the *Guinness Book of Records* to mark their achievement, now on display in the Pie Hall.

The Radio One Goodie Mobile doing a brisk trade on the first pie Sunday.

WORLD RECORD

GUINNESS BOOK
OF RECORDS

THIS IS TO CERTIFY THAT

THE LARGEST MEAT PIE

WEIGHING 9030 kg

WAS THE

9TH DENBY DALE PIE

BAKED ON

3 SEPTEMBER 1988

DONALD McFARLAN   NORRIS McWHIRTER

The pie entered the *Guinness Book of Records* as the biggest meat and potato pie in the world, beating the previous record held by the United States of America, although a somewhat larger apple pie still held the overall record, again made by the Americans.

The event had been expected to raise a large amount of money for local charities and projects, but in fact, initially, made a loss, estimated to be in the region of £40,000. The police launched an official investigation but were unable to find sufficient evidence to warrant further action and on the advice of the Crown Prosecution Service dropped the case. The major problem was that the amount of money that had been banked could not be reconciled with proceeds from portions of pie sold and ticket receipts. Of course the many gatecrashers who avoided the £2 entrance fee to the field did not help matters. The worst aspect of the inquiry was the shadow of suspicion under which the trustee's had to live, particularly considering all their hard work and time. To their credit they overturned the losses and eventually made a profit of £8,000. This was achieved through further sales of memorabilia and the settlement of a dispute over an account with a public relations company. The money was invested in the purchase of Wither Wood at the top of the Gilthwaites housing estate in the village, to preserve it for the community and protect it against any development. This is now managed by the Woodlands Trust. The pie dish itself now forms part of a butterfly garden at Gilthwaites First School, its great girth filled with plants to help create an attractive display.

The garden was opened by children's author Helen Cresswell in 1992.

The 1988 pie dish, photographed in 2011, at Gilthwaites First School, Denby Dale, now used as a huge planter in a butterfly garden.

Chapter 12

2 September 2000

The Millennium Pie

Pie No. 10

A new Millennium – a new pie? The news was greeted by local people with the usual amount of scepticism and disbelief. The main point of interest was that it had only been twelve years since the last record breaker, but although this did indeed seem a hasty gap of years a precedent had been set back in 1896. The embarrassing debacle of the 1887 event had left a bad taste in the mouths of the villagers and they swiftly moved to address the problem only nine years later. This is not to imply that the 1988 event was anything but a huge success but why not a Millennium pie? Although the tradition of roughly one pie a generation was well established the turning of 1999 and the changing of the first number of the year for the first time in a thousand years was something a little bit special. Several members of the 1988 committee had mooted the potential of holding an event this year at the end of the successful 1988 celebrations and Jonas Kenyon had said as much when he opened the Pie Hall in 1972, but time and people had moved on. Besides celebrating the new Millennium the pie coincided with the Queen Mother's 100th birthday and the 150th anniversary of the Penistone Railway Line.

The initial idea originated with a group of friends in February 1999, led by Stuart Imeson, over a few pints in the Dalesman (formerly the Prospect) public house in Denby Dale. Mr Imeson admitted in the Souvenir brochure that:

> Had we not subsequently stumbled across the fine body of individuals, with the array of skill and experience that are involved today I would have to admit that we would soon have been completely out of our depth.

One of the most prominent of these individuals was the man who became chairman of the 2000 Pie Committee, Paul McEnhill, a freelance quantity surveyor. Having a background in oil exploration and construction he had never attended a previous pie event because of his commitments abroad. Stuart Imeson became vice chairman and the rest of the committee was made up of the following: Mary McEnhill, Martyn Siddle, Sue Bridges, Sharon Lyman, Howard Gamble (head chef for the second time), Jill Fletcher, Mike Swithenby and Mike Elliott. The sub-committee comprised: Peter Buckley, Alan Orange, Dawn Charlton, Vicki Bridgemen, Debbie Coldwell and John Kenyon.

On 22 April 1999, it was reported in the *Huddersfield Examiner* that the Denby Dale Pie Millennium Association has formed a committee to organise the making of a pie for the year 2000. The committee described their aims as to continue a long-standing tradition in the village, to raise money for local projects and to provide two wonderful family days out, and they had eighteen months in which to do it. The first problem the committee faced was one of funding and this was overcome in the, by now, usual way of producing merchandise, including the now iconic pie plate. In addition to this a grant of £5,000 was made by the Millennium Festival For All fund.

Paul McEnhill.

Pie 2000 Committee members, left to right: Martyn Siddle, Sue Bridges, Stewart Imeson, Mary McEnhill, Paul McEnhill, Mike Swithenby, Sharon Lyman, Jill Fletcher, Mike Elliott.

A base was established for the Denby Dale Millennium Pie Association at Unit 12d Springfield Mill, Norman Rd, Denby Dale and it was from here that all fundraising activities were co-ordinated.

Following the tradition of each pie being bigger than the last, the committee decided to attempt a new world record. To achieve this a new pie dish was designed by a team from the mechanical engineering department at the University of Huddersfield. Mike Mavromihales and Tony Johnson took advice from Kirklees Environmental Health Department as they drew up a dish 40 feet long, 9 feet wide and 3 feet deep, capable of holding 12 tonnes of pie. It should be said that Kirklees Environmental Health were most supportive of the whole venture, and without their support throughout the planning, cooking and distribution stages of organising the pie the day very well may never have happened.

The Millennium Pie Logo.

The dish was constructed by Parkway Sheet Metal Works at Rotherham. The company was owned by pie sub-committee member Peter Buckley. Peter grew up at Dry Hill Farm, where the 1964 pie event was held and when he was involved with the preparations. As with the pies of 1964 and 1988, the pie dish was also the pie oven. This time it was split into twenty-four compartments, each having a three-kilowatt heating element, which could be individually controlled. ADS Johnson supplied the mild steel to make an outer frame, which weighed one tonne. The heating elements, silicone wiring, switchgear, canopy, extraction fan and double outer sheet added another tonne to the weight of the empty dish. The

The pie dish under construction at Peter Buckley's, Parkway Sheet Metal Works in Rotherham. *(Susan Buckley collection.)*

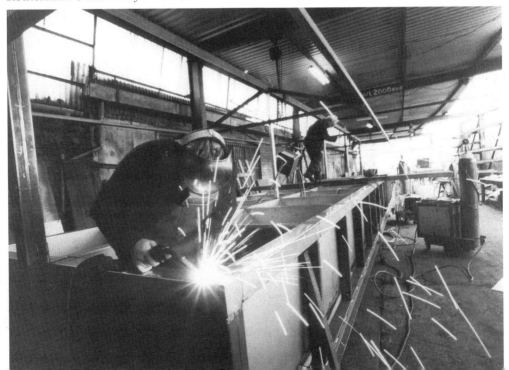

Peter Buckley standing in one of the twenty-four cooking compartments of the 2000 pie dish. *(Susan Buckley collection.)*

compartments and lids were made from stainless steel supplied by Avesta of Sheffield. In total, the pie dish cost around £37,000 to make.

Whilst the dish was being created the committee had to concern themselves with parking facilities. Visitors would be asked to use the park-and-ride services, which were to be made available on the day. Spaces for 2,500 cars were available in a car park off Fall Edge Lane, between Upper Denby and Ingbirchworth, and a further 3,334 spaces could be utilised at the old Emley showground near Clayton West. The park-and-ride cost £2 with buses running to Denby Dale every few minutes. Car parks near the pie field included Denby Hall Farm, 3,000 spaces and Miller Hill car park with 180 spaces.

Entertainment had also to be provided. The procession was to include the newly chosen pie queen, twelve-year-old Amy Collick and her assistant, six-year-old Ross Charlton. The order of the parade was:

Hade Edge Brass Band
Pie Vehicle
Crofton Majorettes
Shire Horses
Denby Dale Brownies and Guides
Sheffield Giants Stiltwalkers and Band

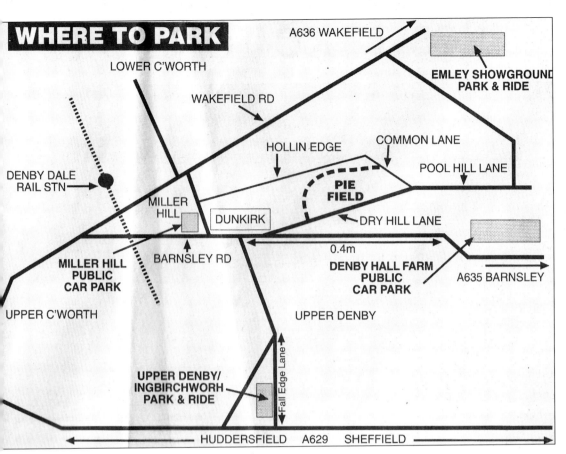

WHERE TO PARK

A636 WAKEFIELD

LOWER C'WORTH

EMLEY SHOWGROUND
PARK & RIDE

WAKEFIELD RD

HOLLIN EDGE

COMMON LANE

POOL HILL LANE

DENBY DALE
RAIL STN

PIE
FIELD

MILLER
HILL

DUNKIRK

DRY HILL LANE

0.4m

MILLER HILL
PUBLIC
CAR PARK

BARNSLEY RD

DENBY HALL FARM
PUBLIC
CAR PARK

A635 BARNSLEY

UPPER C'WORTH

UPPER DENBY

UPPER DENBY/
INGBIRCHWORH
PARK & RIDE

Fall Edge Lane

HUDDERSFIELD   A629   SHEFFIELD

Map detailing the park and ride operation.

Denby Dale Scouts and Cubs
Spicebird Fire-eaters
Clayton West Cubs
Keith Stone & Pennine Jazzmen
Cawthorne Brass Band
Gilthwaites School Dragon

Also taking part in the parade was Tom Owen, son of Bill Owen (who starred as Compo in the long-running BBC light comedy series *Last of the Summer Wine*). He travelled in a vintage *Last of the Summer Wine* tour bus and was also chosen to crown the pie queen Amy Collick at 2:00pm prior to distribution of the pie.

The committee decided to continue with the precedent set by the 1988 event and have a two-day show. Hector Buckley once again stepped in, this time with the offer of enough land at Dry Hill Farm to stage the event on. He was now becoming almost as much a part of the event as the pie itself.

A fairground, including the world's oldest steam-driven carousel, street performers, vintage cars, quad bikes, craft stalls, food and bars were all to be on offer in the pie field along with a main arena for entertainments such as the Crofton Majorettes and an inter-pub tug-of-war competition.

A large main stage was also erected, provided by Bradford Raise the Roof it was to be the centrepiece of the occasion. This was to provide a base for a Home Radio Roadshow to be broadcast from here, interspersed with performances from Cawthorne and Scissett Youth brass bands and guest presenters. The compere on ie day was Paedar Long. The entertainment line up for Sunday consisted of a number of tribute acts including: The Bootleg Bee Gees, Andrew Browning as George Michael, Kings of Queen, Paul Warren as Robbie Williams and Mamma Mia an Abba tribute. The headline act, which began at 8:15pm were the Woolpackers consisting of Alun Lewis and Billy Hartman, stars of the television soap *Emmerdale*, who played a rousing country music set.

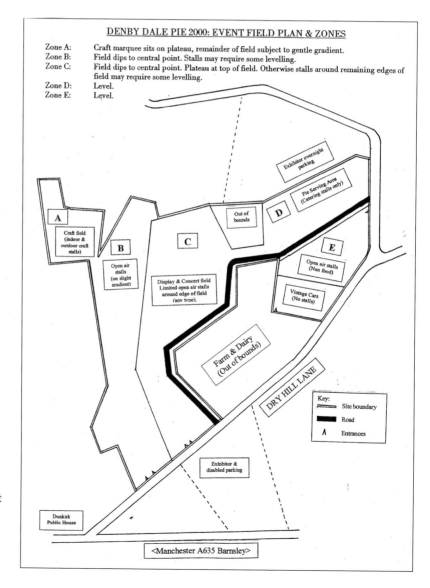

DENBY DALE PIE 2000: EVENT FIELD PLAN & ZONES

Zone A: Craft marquee sits on plateau, remainder of field subject to gentle gradient.
Zone B: Field dips to central point. Stalls may require some levelling.
Zone C: Field dips to central point. Plateau at top of field. Otherwise stalls around remaining edges of field may require some levelling.
Zone D: Level.
Zone E: Level.

Map of the venue for the celebrations at Dry Hill.

The actual cooking of the pie was to take place inside a huge marquee at the end of the pie field. A large extractor fan built into the roof of the pie dish took much of the steam out of the tent. The ingredients (including beer for the first time) in order to try and break the world record were:

4,864kg beef, 3,786kg water, 2,233kg potatoes, 1,008kg onions,
164kg John Smiths bitter, 105kg herbs

The pie was expected to take about twelve hours to cook. As with the previous two pies, the crust that was to adorn it on its parade around the village was to be thrown away as inedible, in accordance with health and safety rules, once the pie had reached the field where it was to be carved up. This dummy crust was made of sponge at Manor Bakeries of Barnsley, the company continuing its support for the Denby Dale pie from where they had left off in 1988. Manor Bakeries are responsible for, amongst other well-known brands, Mr Kipling's cakes and Lyons foodstuffs. The head chef of 1988, Howard Gamble, was again recruited from Manor Bakeries along with ten assistants to cook the Millennium pie.

Mr Gamble, involved with catering since 1971, was by now getting used to the responsibility:

I was nervous last time in case it went wrong and I got egg on my face. It's a lot of responsibility. The committee have put in a lot of work to get to this stage, but everybody remembers what the pie tastes like. Last time we had no extractor fan and the steam kept tripping all the electricity out. This year we have an extractor fan built in and the dish is stainless steel with a non-stick coating.

To be able to supply a piece of crust with each portion of pie a team of twenty-five bakers worked on a pastry mixture for eight hours in order to create 60,000 individual portions to be distributed at serving time. Manor Bakeries generously donated the crusts and labour they supplied for the Denby Dale charities, which were being supported by the committee.

Howard Gamble, the chef in charge of the cooking operation for the second time.

A crisis occurred during the final month of the build-up to pie day. Local farmers had originally offered to supply the meat for the pie, but they had not realised at the time they made the promise that the pie was to be so much bigger than any before. A decline in the industry and falling beef prices did not help the situation and an extra £12,000 of beef was needed to make up the shortfall. A saviour was found in the shape of supermarket giant ASDA, who donated six tonnes of British beef from their organic supplier, Dawn Meats.

Ex Coldstream guard Raymond Haigh was again called upon to 'guard' the pie during the cooking procedure. By now a veteran of the 1964 and 1988 bakes, Raymond's initial response was:

Don't you think I'm a bit too old for the job?

But seventy-year-old Raymond did indeed accept the committee's offer to provide overnight security, but only upon the condition that he was in charge and every official was to understand that:

> *If their name's not on my list, they won't get in. It's as simple as that. I have a 100% success record and I don't intend to break it now!*

By 31 August, the fields on Dry Hill Lane were filling up with marquees, fences and roped-off areas. Electricity supplies were installed and seventy-six toilets arrived on the site. In total £35,543 was charged for preparing the pie field and transport.

Pie field manager, Mike Swithenby said:

> *On Saturday it looked like a nightmare after all the rain, but it has dried out now and is looking good.*

Ex Coldstream Guard, Raymond Haigh, on security duties for the third time.

Baking began at 1:40am on the Saturday morning and by 11:00am the pie was pronounced cooked and ready. It was loaded onto a 31 tonne lorry owned by A P Hollingworth, a company based in Cumberworth, which provided the vehicle and its

Howard Gamble adds more meat to the mixture. *(Susan Buckley collection.)*

Howard Gamble suggests that he is happy with proceedings. *(Susan Buckley collection.)*

The sponge crust is fitted to the top of the dish, made solely for the parade it was discarded after the opening ceremony. *(Susan Buckley collection.)*

driver free of charge for the day. The vehicle was driven by fifty-seven year-old Selwyn Croft of Denby Dale who commented that:

> *I've been a lorry driver all my life and I've carried some abnormal loads, but this was my first pie!*

The pie was taken from Dry Hill to the official start line for the parade, at the Dalesman public house, which began at 12:30pm. Led by Hade Edge Brass Band and followed by fire-eaters, stiltwalkers and many others in a colourful procession, the pie made its way along Wakefield Road before turning off up Miller Hill and back to Dry Hill Lane, a duration of forty-five minutes. Queues were quick to form in the pie field, though under grey skies, but the rain held off.

Map of the pie parade route.

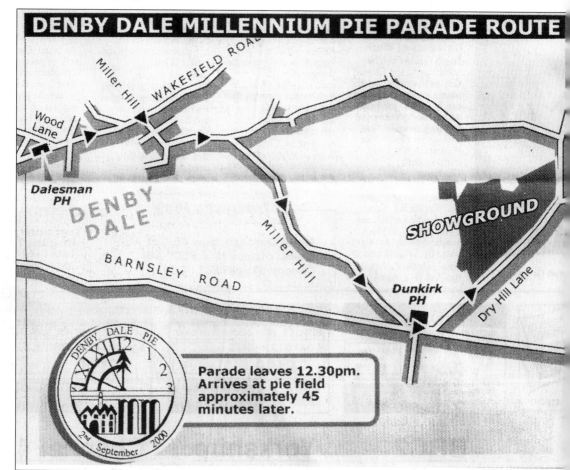

The pie travels along Wakefield Road through the centre of Denby Dale. *(Huddersfield Examiner.)*

The pie makes its way towards Miller Hill on Wakefield Road. *(Huddersfield Examiner.)*

The band in the procession at the bottom of Miller Hill, passing the site of the old corn mill where three previous pies were baked. *(Susan Buckley collection.)*

The pie vehicle just past Rombpickle on Miller Hill.

Almost back to Dry Hill, the pie leads the parade.

Sheffield Giants Stiltwalkers follow the pie.

The Pennine Jazz Men float on Miller Hill.

The parade continues to make its way towards Dry Hill.

The crowds follow the procession up Miller Hill towards the Dunkirk.

Before the pie was cut the Bishop of Wakefield, the Rt Rev Nigel McCullough, gave a blessing and told the audience:

> *May he who fed 5,000*
> *The Lord ascended high*
> *Today bless 50,000*
> *And this Millennium pie*
>
> *And grant that in years to come*
> *They'll often tell the tale*
> *Of how the pie world record*
> *Was broken at Denby Dale.*

In a break with tradition the committee had decided to opt for a non-Daler to make the first ceremonial cut into the pie. The man chosen for the job was Harold Dennis Bird, better known as the cricket umpire 'Dickie' Bird. On accepting the role he said:

I am really looking forward to opening the festival. I like a nice piece of pie. I think it is the oddest job I have ever been asked to do – people all over the world ask me to do things for them, but this will be special. Denby Dale pie is renowned throughout the world and I am very pleased to be involved with such an old tradition, especially in Millennium year.

Dickie's involvement in pre-publicity for the pie had extended to a photograph opportunity, when he and pie queen, Amy Collick had posed in the dish when it was floated upon the canal outside its place of birth, Parkway Sheet Metal Works, Rotherham, to test it for leaks.

Dickie Bird and pie queen Amy Collick aboard the floating pie dish. (*Susan Buckley collection.*)

The pie dish being floated on the canal to test it for leaks. (*Susan Buckley collection.*)

Dickie Bird makes the first ceremonial cut into the Millennium pie. (*Huddersfield Examiner.*)

Dickie Bird enjoying his portion of pie.
(*Susan Buckley collection.*)

Unfortunately on this occasion there was no ceremonial knife and fork, though Mr Bird did use an antique Kaskara sword, associated with nineteenth century Sudanese warriors.

Forty-five minutes after the pie's arrival in the field, a large team of volunteers wearing 'Denby Dale Pie 2000' t-shirts began to serve more than 22,000 (some reports suggest 30,000) people with a portion of the pie and Dickie Bird was impressed:

> It was delicious but then again I knew it would be. I called it the eighth wonder of the world but only in Yorkshire could we do something like this. The people of Denby Dale should be very proud.

Local historian, ninety-year-old William Herbert Senior, who was a member of the 1928 Pie Committee and had attended the pies of 1964 and 1988, said:

> Today has been wonderful and the organisers really need to be congratulated.

Tom Owen remarked that:

> *It is absolutely brilliant but it is such a shame that Dad (Bill Owen) could not be here to see it because I know he would have been very impressed.*

Finally, head chef Howard Gamble's verdict:

> *I thought the gravy could have been a bit thicker, but I had to put in more meat and less potato than I would in a normal pie. It was a tiring day for the eight of us who had to start baking the pie at 1:30am, but on the whole, everyone seemed pleased with the way it tasted.*

Howard Gamble ladles the pie mixture into crates which were then taken to the servers for distribution. *(Susan Buckley collection.)*

Distribution continues inside the cooking tent. *(Susan Buckley collection.)*

The servers wait for their crates to be filled with pie. *(Susan Buckley collection.)*

The servers in action as the public queue up. *(Susan Buckley collection.)*

The queues continue to form and keep the servers busy. *(Susan Buckley collection.)*

More pie mixture is loaded into crates using the huge ladles employed for the job. *(Susan Buckley collection.)*

In order to keep the fields at Dry Hill clean and tidy a handy local group known as the Green Kleen team began work within minutes of the pie being served, bagging up the rubbish. Leftover pie also had to be removed, indeed, so big was the pie that almost half of it had to be thrown away. Environmental experts were called in to take away the remaining mixture from the dish, which was to be recycled for animal feed.

On the main stage on Sunday, Mama Mia, the Abba tribute act.

All the fun of the fair, the entertainment continues on into Sunday.

The pie dish on the Sunday, its duties not yet over.

The pie dish attracted visitors on the Sunday, keen to see how it was constructed.

224

The pie beat the previous world record for a meat pie of 10 tonnes, set by a group of pie-lovers from Kentucky Fried Chicken in New York in 1995. It also surmounted the efforts of a steak and kidney pie made at Clevedon Football Club on the outskirts of Bristol. This pie was made by a team of seventeen chefs from Stratford-upon-Avon College, in a dish measuring 32 feet by 7 feet and weighing 10.54 tonnes. The problem with this pie was that although Guinness ratified the record, the actual pie was inedible, which makes this claim for a world record tenuous at best.

On pie day itself, the *Guinness Book of Records* was still to confirm the new record but the organisers were not expecting any problems.

Two trading standards officers, Tony Cripps and Paul Downham, had verified and weighed the ingredients. West Yorkshire Trading Standards spokesman Graham Hebblethwaite was to draft a letter for the Pie Committee to confirm that as far as he was concerned the Millennium pie was authentically the biggest pie in the world, a statement backed up by Alan Sherwood of Kirklees Environmental Services.

Unfortunately this early confidence was later shattered. In October, the officials from the *Guinness Book of Records* informed the team behind the Millennium pie that they had failed and that the record was still in the hands of Stratford College. The Millennium pie organisers kept to the conditions imposed upon them by Guinness before the event, but then Guinness quibbled over the content of the pie and the way it was baked. Vice chairman Stuart Imeson explained:

> First they said we had not included pastry in our weights so there was less than 40% meat content, but the pastry was inedible and not included in previous records. The next letter said it was not cooked as a pie – but original details specified nothing about cooking methods. West Yorkshire Trading Standards verified the meat content at 40%.

The 2000 Denby Dale pie had been made using exactly the same rules laid down by Guinness officials that were followed by the bakers of the Stratford pie and indeed the 1988 Denby Dale pie, which was confirmed as a world record at the time. Inexplicably, the 12.10 tonne, 40 feet by 9 feet wide monster created at Denby Dale was never ratified. Guinness has never offered a satisfactory explanation to Denby Dale of their refusal to do so. Surely, to claim a world record the end product has to be edible, unlike the Stratford attempt, otherwise the cooking procedure is at fault and the claim to have baked a pie becomes intangible. The Denby Dale Millennium Pie Committee had no such worries because of the time and effort they put in to make sure this was not the case. Official or not, on 2 September 2000, the world record for the biggest meat pie in the world was broken at the village of Denby Dale.

By late October 2000 the benefit to the local community and the success of the Millennium pie festival was announced in the local press. The profits from the two-day extravaganza totalled £23,587. Chairman Paul McEnhill stated that the committee now planned to invest the profits into the local community.

The Millennium pie dish was not abandoned and forgotten after its first moment of glory. Later in September it was offered to the troubled Millennium Dome on the Greenwich Peninsula, south-east London, now known as the O2 Arena. A Dome spokesman said that many people were asking for the things to be put on display in the Dome but the problem was finding the space. Talks were also held with the organisers of the Wakefield Rhubarb Festival, at the suggestion of ASDA, with regard to using the dish to make a giant rhubarb crumble. In August 2002 the dish came to prominence again. Sited in the ASDA car park at its store on Bradford Road, Brackenhall, Huddersfield, it took just forty minutes to make a world-record-setting toad-in-the-hole. A technical hitch meant the pudding was trimmed down to 4 feet from 8 feet but as no world record existed there was none to beat. The dish included 600 sausages.

The dish still exists, kept on a private land on a farm in the Denby Dale area; its time may even yet not be over.

Rumours of a new pie become more frequent when an event of national importance arises, and, when a slightly younger generation have had the chance to wonder what all the fuss was about. As I write the year 2012 approaches, a year in which Queen Elizabeth II will celebrate her diamond jubilee and the first summer Olympic Games since 1908 will take place in Great Britain. Is this reason enough for a Denby Dale Pie? Perhaps the next major occasion for the event would more likely be the coronation of King Charles III (or George VII depending upon which name he chooses).

Is there still a place for a Denby Dale pie in the twenty-first century? Carnivals and fetes, village parties of any sort are now much rarer occasions than ever. The lack of street parties held in the district on the occasion of Prince William and Kate Middleton's marriage in 2011 serves to illustrate this decline in support for entertainment that many now perceive as old-fashioned. Yet the mere mention of the possibility of a new monster pie bake in Denby Dale serves to set tongues wagging. Newspapers and television companies fall over themselves in order to cover proceedings and business companies make overtures to the cause in order to publicise themselves. Indeed, even in fallow years when there is no talk of a pie in the village, independent television producers still look upon Denby Dale as an ideal place to make their programmes. In February 2011 the Hairy Bikers of BBC cookery fame filmed in the village, to be followed in April by The Great British Bake Off, again a BBC cookery programme.

The difficulties of making a new pie even bigger than the last also increase with each passing year. Health and safety issues, financing the cost of a giant cooking dish and simply the expense of buying all the ingredients, particularly the meat, are reasons enough to deter even the bravest of hearts. But all this has been said before, and all this has been done before, and each time, against all expectation, bigger and better than the last time.

One thing seems certain, the village tradition has not died, it is simply laying dormant, an almost mythological monster of immense proportions, which appears maybe only once a generation, roused by the voices of a fanatical (and some would say idiotic) few. As the monster rises like a phoenix from the embers of the last pie it begins to spread its wings, the voices increase, breeding cherished memories of bygone days, until the clamour is almost deafening and the village of Denby Dale can only slay the beast by baking another pie.

Chapter 13

Pie Memorabilia

Among the many interesting and unique features included in the baking of a Denby Dale pie, is the merchandise made commercially available to raise funds in order to account for expenses in the planning and organisation and also to aid eventual profits. Alongside this are the numerous non-commercial souvenirs collected by the public, legally or otherwise, which have passed down from generation to generation as heirlooms, many becoming not only collectible but also valuable throughout those years.

The *Huddersfield Examiner* August, 1928:

RELICS OF THE GREAT DENBY DALE PIE - Sold by Auction:

In Denby Dale Council School, the relics of the great Carnival Pie, utensils that were used in its making and a number of other lots associated with the effort for the Huddersfield Royal Infirmary, were offered for sale by public auction. Mr G H Wilby was the auctioneer, but there was little conventional about the sale. No restrictions were read out and the Incorporated Law Society was not called to witness. The rule appeared to be that the highest bidder was most certainly the buyer. The first article offered was a large tin bath. About this the auctioneer waxed eloquent. 'Was it not used in the most stupendous effort that has ever been made in Denby Dale on behalf of charity?' he asked. But the bids came slowly. After all, a large tin bath, however useful it may be as a bath, is hardly the thing people choose as a souvenir. But then the auctioneer pointed out that in this very bath, part of the great pie had been carried before being served to the waiting thousands. That did it, and Mr Arthur Brook acquired the lot for 6s 9d. Next came an artistic metal vessel, decorated in simple manner in white and blue enamel. People with no poetry in their souls called it a tin bowl but Mr Wilby asked that this lot should not be priced as if it were being bought in a shop. This too had associations with the pie that added many times to its value. Mrs Blamires parted with 3s 6d. 'Ladles, three assorted' was the next item and the first ones to be put up complete with handles. 'This,' said the auctioneer, 'simply wants a little decoration, and then think of its value as a decorative article in any front room. What will it be worth in a hundred years time?' 'Yes, what?' somebody asked doubtfully. But bidding commenced briskly and rose rapidly from 1s to £1 when they were sold to Mr W

Dewhirst. This was the highest price raised by a single article during the sale. Smaller ladles were then offered for 6s apiece. Six shillings was also the price realised for the dripping tin, which still bore the marks of its encounter with the giant pie, and which the connoisseurs who were present had to admit was indeed beautifully marked. Several real gems which were eagerly sought by the bidders had been saved until the latter part of the sale. There was a perfect specimen of a paper doyley, in all probability of the early Woolworth dynasty. Upon this doyley the first piece of pie was served, and on it too was to be seen the mark of the time. Mrs Jonas Kenyon was the purchaser at 2s 6d. Mrs Kenyon was presented with a meat hook used in fastening the muslin over the edges of the pie in recognition of her services. By this time interest had begun to flag, but everybody revived when the auctioneer announced that he had to offer a cricket bat, won as a boy by Mr Harry Turton at the sports in connection with the baking of the Jubilee pie in 1887. This fetched 14s and a programme of events for the same celebrations made 7s 6d. When a signed agenda, calling together a meeting in connection with the barrel organ collections, was sold to a gentleman from another village, there was almost as great a sensation as when the manuscript of Alice in Wonderland *was knocked down to an American buyer some months ago. Then there was the half of the paste medallion, which the auctioneer described as forming 'the culminating point of the whole structure', in other words, it was the piece of crust which was situated in the middle of the pie. It was sold with a certificate certifying it to be genuine, and signed by the five ladies who placed it there on the great day. Mr Jubb, who was the buyer, estimated the value of the piece of crust at 4s., and the signatures of the ladies at sixpence. Several people were disappointed that they could not secure bargains, but none more so than the man who spoke to me at the door. 'I'm sorry that they didn't put up the dish for sale' he said.*

'Why?' I asked,

'Well, I wanted a pond for my ducks,' was his reply.

The things that people will pay good money for! The term 'Piemania' had been coined, and it would certainly appear to have begun at least this far back, but then consider again the amount of crusts or slices that have been preserved by local families for years.

During the chaos of 1846 trophy hunters were in action, as the pie was being torn to shreds and trampled underfoot, some far-sighted individuals managed to grab pieces of the crust, which have been preserved to this day. Similarly, pieces also survive from 1887, 1896, 1928 and 1964. Indeed, local farmer, Mr Tom Lodge, was featured on the BBC documentary of 1988 at his then home, Toby Wood farm, where he proudly removed from his freezer a piece of the 1964 pie, retained from that day. It may sound weird to the outsider, but owning a piece of a bygone pie is a prestigious accolade to be treasured and revered. Indeed, when asked by children or outsiders the locals would invariably give the wrong directions as to the location of the 'grave' of the Jubilee pie, so as to prevent them digging up a piece to keep as a souvenir for themselves.

As we have seen, items associated with the advertising, cooking or distribution of a pie were also highly-prized, banners, signposts, tickets, cutlery, bunting, you name it, and you can almost guarantee that somewhere, something has survived. Indeed, an apron alleged to have been used in 1788 was featured on the *Tonight* documentary in 1963.

It was in 1887 that the beginnings of a by now, well-established tradition took root. The first pie plate was produced, bearing a portrait of Queen Victoria in the centre and having the words: *Souvenir, Denby Dale Pie, 8 feet diameter and 2 feet deep, Queen's Jubilee 1887* and the date *August 27 1887* emblazoned on it. Produced to promote and celebrate a successful day, they were balanced by the 'funeral cards' printed hurriedly for its burial in Toby Wood, three days after the event. A fair number of these funeral cards survive but are highly sought after by collectors of pie souvenirs. Astonishingly, another plate was produced for the Resurrection pie a week later. Now a very rare commodity, these plates bore two portraits of the Queen, one as she was at the beginning of her reign and the other as she was at the time of the baking of the pie. These plates sold well, but one could speculate that their rarity today could be due to low production numbers caused by time constraints.

Pie plates were now coming thick and fast, another was produced for the celebrations of 1896. These were similar in concept, though the portrait of Queen Victoria was now replaced by

The fist commemorative plate ever produced for the first of the 1887 pies.

Produced only a week later for the Resurrection pie, this plate is now very rare.

One of the wooden 1887 pie spoons used by the servers, now on display at the Pie Hall.

a painting of a pie, which looked very like a pork pie of today. The words around the rim were *Denby Dale, Jubilee Pie In Commemoration of the Repeal of the Corn Laws 1846*. Also produced was a silver brooch, more commonly referred to as a 'pie pin'. It is unknown at present how many of these were made; a local newspaper cutting reported the following in 1988:

> *Miscellany has had another couple of calls about the silver pie pins issued to mark the 1896 Denby Dale pie. One lady phoned to say that her family had kept a pin in a button box, but it was now resting in a safer place. She understood that three pins were made at the time. But then a lady wrote from Bradford to say that she also had a pin which, like the others, had been handed down from older members of the family. So we are now wondering just how many pie pins were made.*

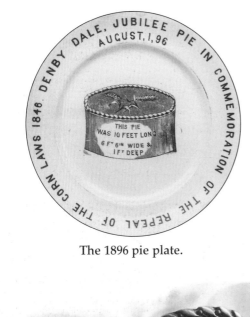

The 1896 pie plate.

A section of a display of memorabilia at the Pie Hall, featuring two old serving ladles.

A pie brooch, actual length just over 2cm.

The answer to this is certainly more than three. I possess one myself, and the article obviously makes reference to others still in existence. The brooch itself was fashioned into the shape of a pie, surrounded by a neat floral design. It gives the date of the pie and its dimensions and it is to be wondered just how many more still survive, buried in button boxes or packed away in drawers or lofts. Perhaps these were made purely for members of the committee in recognition of their services that year. Programmes were also issued, priced at one penny each; the single page gave details about the contents of the pie, its dimensions and its weight, along with entertainment for the day.

The 1928 pie plate adopted a similar theme to that of its predecessor, a glazed white plate with the words, *Denby Dale Pie In Aid of the Huddersfield Royal Infirmary*. In the middle was another painting of a pie (though this one was steaming hot) and of course the all important dimensions. A special edition of the plate was made for the committee members, baring an inner border of red, blue and green leaves as well as the design described above. A number of special dinner services were also manufactured, with oval meat dishes, covered tureens and gravy boats all bearing the steaming pie design. The latter along with the special edition plate are now very rare and much sought after by collectors.

The 1928 pie plate.

Also in existence from this time are many printed poems and songs, composed to celebrate the days events in verse, such as the following which was to be sung to the tune of *There is a Happy Land*,

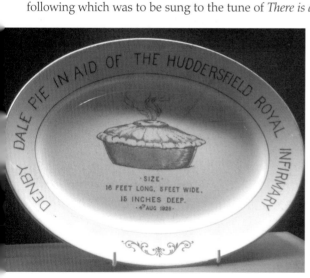

An oval meat dish dating from 1928.

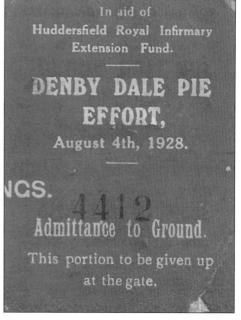

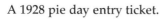

A 1928 pie day entry ticket.

Of Denby Woodland Dale,
List to the tale,
When came the costly Rail,
Named Denby Dale,
Viaduct made of wood,
The design neat and work good,
To carry folks and coal,
A boon to all.

Thirty years was its trail,
Then it did fail,
So stone it had to be,
As you can see,
T'Pie at Denby Dale
Crowds will come by bus and rail,
And these songs on 4th prox,
Will rock the 'Docks'.

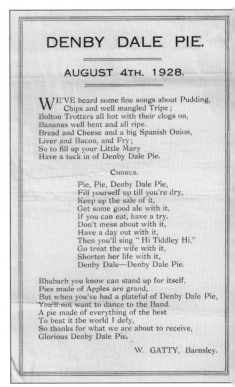

DENBY DALE PIE.

AUGUST 4TH. 1928.

WE'VE heard some fine songs about Pudding,
Chips and well mangled Tripe;
Bolton Trotters all hot with their clogs on,
Bananas well bent and all ripe.
Bread and Cheese and a big Spanish Onion,
Liver and Bacon, and Fry;
So to fill up your Little Mary
Have a tuck in of Denby Dale Pie.

CHORUS.

Pie, Pie, Denby Dale Pie,
Fill yourself up till you're dry,
Keep up the sale of it,
Get some good ale with it,
If you can eat, have a try.
Don't mess about with it,
Have a day out with it,
Then you'll sing "Hi Tiddley Hi,"
Go treat the wife with it,
Shorten her life with it,
Denby Dale—Denby Dale Pie.

Rhubarb you know can stand up for itself,
Pies made of Apples are grand,
But when you've had a plateful of Denby Dale Pie,
You'll not want to dance to the Band.
A pie made of everything of the best
To beat it the world I defy,
So thanks for what we are about to receive,
Glorious Denby Dale Pie.

W. GATTY, Barnsley.

An example of a printed song sheet from 1928.

The printed sheet contained two other songs and cost 1d each, the proceeds all going towards the total to be given to the Huddersfield Royal Infirmary, they were printed by Hirst Buckley of Scissett.

Memorabilia also exists from the auction and subsequent meltdown of the 1887/1896 pie dish, from 1940. The large red, black and blue posters advertising the event have survived in some homes and businesses, indeed posters and banners from previous and subsequent celebrations are again treasured items. As we have already seen, a few rusted pieces of the dish were sold separately at the auction, the purchasers being allowed to retain them, though it would seem that only one of these pieces still survives.

The 1964 Pie Committee were well aware of the marketing potential of the pie in order to finance the days proceedings. The by now established tradition of producing a commemorative plate was duly continued, supplied by Britannia Designs Ltd, of Townstal Pottery, Dartmouth, Devon. The design was selected by a competition and once the winner was chosen the committee placed orders for large quantities. By July about 7,000 had already been sold and by August the sales committee wrote in *Pie News* that if you hadn't already bought your pie plate, 'don't leave it too late'.

The pottery have told the committee, in reply to their request for further stocks of plates, that they are unable to produce any more before pie day, and it is the general policy that once 5 September is over no more will be ordered, otherwise this job of selling could go on forever. The despatching deptment are at present getting off an order for 750 plates. The company who has ordered these will send them out to their own customers throughout the world and attached to each one will be a calendar for 1965.

The 1964 pie plate.

Almost, but not quite, one of the runners up in the 1964 pie plate design competition.

A Christmas card produced in 1963 to generate funds for the Pie Committee.

A half pint glazed tankard from 1963.

A glazed 1964 pie brooch.

The committee was also despatching plates by post to all parts of the world and was pleased to report that only one had arrived broken with only a month to go before the big day. Alongside the plates a limited edition tankard was produced, small and large they sold for 10s and 17s 6d each. A booklet was produced under the direction of Mrs Nora Kitson entitled *The Mammoth Pies of Denby Dale*, priced at 3s, and these amongst other items were available to the public at most local shops which had been appointed to sell the souvenirs. Mugs, brooches, dinner services and the like added to the list of items available this year. Naylor Brothers Clayware even manufactured a small, brown salt-glazed pie dish that featured a representation of a clay drainage pipe in the bottom of the bowl with their name carved upon it. A special edition of these was made exclusively for members of the various Pie Committees, replacing the pipe with the individual's name.

For the day of the pie itself, a souvenir brochure was produced, priced 2s 6d. This featured many interesting adverts for companies that have long since ceased trading. Also included was a full history of pie making in the village, written by publicity officer John Netherwood and other interesting articles concerning the preparations for that year's happy event.

Glazed pie dish produced by Naylor Brothers in 1964.

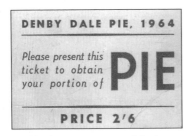

1964 pie event entry ticket.

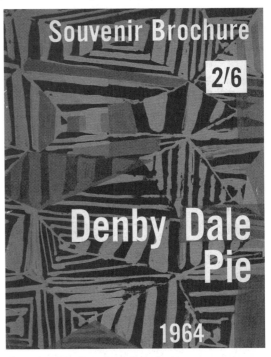

The 1964 Pie Souvenir brochure.

After a gap of eight years, further memorabilia was produced to celebrate the opening of the Pie Hall in 1972. Commemorative glassware was commissioned, bearing the dates of previous pies as well as the date of this important event. Further plates were also produced, featuring the 1964 design but including the words *Commemorating the opening of the Pie Hall built with the proceeds of the 1964 Pie.* The 1972 version was produced with a maroon coloured design on a white background. A year later an anniversary edition of the plate was produced in yellow, variations of blue and green were also made.

A plate to commemorate the opening of the Pie Hall in 1972.

An anniversary issue of the plate commemorating the opening of the Pie Hall.

A wine glass produced to commemorate the opening of the Pie Hall.

By 1988 the era of commercialism had been in place for some time and once the decision had been taken to bake another pie in 1987, the call for commemorative memorabilia went wild. Committee member Stan Ward fashioned an eye-catching logo, which was to feature on all official pie memorabilia. Once more the design for the pie plates was decided by having a competition. Mr J Pearson of Penistone beat over seventy other entries and his design was printed on over 30,000 plates by Johnson Bothers, part of the Waterford-Wedgewood group in Stoke-on-Trent. The *Pie Report* gave the following details:

Using a hand engraving method from a copper plate, the decoration will be under glazed to ensure that it is dishwasher and microwave safe. The shape is traditional sovereign and the plate is of the finest quality earthenware and will be produced in blue and white.

For pre-paid advance orders the cost of a plate was £7.50, until 1 June when the cost was to rise to £8.50, but this was not the only one available this year. A plate had already been commissioned to commemorate the launch night back in 1987, it was a limited edition and bore the pie logo in gold, these and mugs were purchased from Hornsea Pottery. Also produced was a plate given to the servers in recognition of their hard work, the total now up to three.

The 1988 pie plate.

The 1988 Coalport produced plate, designed by John Ball.

The 1988 Goss China sepia plate, designed by John Ball.

A plate was also produced by Goss China in Stoke on Trent, which featured a sepia design, by John Ball depicting aspects of previous pie celebrations. Royal Worcester produced a further 9-inch pie dish bearing the same design. Sold exclusively through the Peter Jones china shops, the plate retailed at £12.50 and the dish £13.50.

Also commissioned by the Denby Dale Pie Trust from Peter Jones was a limited edition colour plate, which was produced by Coalport. John Ball was again responsible for the artwork on the 10-inch plate, which retailed at £40.00. These are now collectors items as only 2,000 were produced, were sold from Peter Jones outlets and were also available in the pie field on pie day at the Peter Jones stand. The polystyrene dishes, which would be used to serve up the pie, bore a design chosen from entries by local schoolchildren, and so, in 1988, everyone had a chance to be a part of history.

By the time of the official launch night hats, balloons, pens and stickers had been ordered. These were followed by mugs, matches, glassware, combs, key rings and postcards. A local company, Cellarchoice, supplied wine from the Loire Valley in France, both red and white wines hit the market contained in specially designed bottles. Instead of paper labels, the history of Pie Madness and the Pie 1988 logo were enamelled onto the bottles, and again, many have been kept as souvenirs.

A song was also recorded for the big day. Written and performed by local close harmony group, Take Five it was paired with the Holmfirth Anthem, *Pratty Flowers*, although not a serious challenger for a number one position in the pop charts, it added to the growing stacks of memorabilia already available in fine style.

Two books were also written locally born David Bostwick, who for many years was honorary curator of pie memorabilia on behalf of the Pie Hall, wrote an illustrated history of the pies, and also aided in television and radio publicity. Children's author Helen Cresswell had her story *The Piemakers* based on the history of the pie, re-issued by publishers Faber & Faber to coincide with the 1988 event. All the latter, along with cuddly toys and sweatshirts were sold from the Pie 1988 shop at Springfield Mills in the village from December 1987.

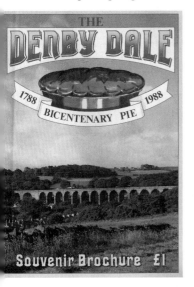

Souvenir Brochure £1

Souvenir 1988 pie mug.

The 1988 souvenir programme.

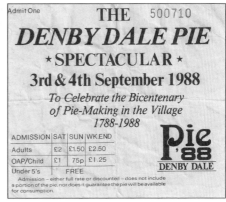

Pie 1988 field entry ticket.

Of course certain individuals and companies were unable to miss the opportunity to cash in on such a well-known event and some merchandise was produced and sold purely for profit. The committee accepted that it was difficult to take action against these opportunists, but urged the public to only buy items bearing the official Pie 1988 logo, thus ensuring that the money would find its way back into the village and not into an individual's pocket.

From the day itself napkins sponsored by Warburton's, seasoning sponsored by Nestlé, carrier bags sponsored by Naylor Bros. and sauce sponsored by Hammond's alongside dozens of other items were kept by a mindful public knowing only too well the value of pie relics. The souvenir brochure, priced £1, and even the tickets for entry into the field were kept alongside other more dubious items. Temporary bus stop signs, bunting, police cones, public notices, road closed signs and other more general signposts were collected by a voracious public, determined to possess something special to remind them of this unique day.

The Millennium Pie Committee had a hard act to follow but rose to the challenge magnificently. Alongside the traditional pie plate (£12.50) a limited edition plate was also commissioned, retailing at £24. An engraved tankard (£25), goblet (£25), mug and paperweight, were also available. Following in the successful wake of 1988, three wines were also made available for sale known as *Vin de Pie'*. The wines, all from the south of France, were organised and sold by Springfield Wines.

The 2000 pie plate.

A collectable limited edition pie plate from 2000.

A pint glass engraved with the Pie 2000 logo.

The Millennium Pie Souvenir Programme.

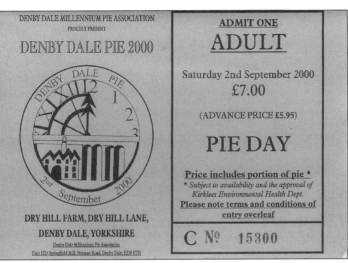

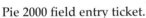

Pie 2000 field entry ticket.

A bottle of Denby D'Ale beer, produced for the 2000 pie celebrations.

As this was the first Denby Dale pie to feature beer in the recipe it was deemed appropriate that an addition should be made to the ranks of the increasingly popular real ale market. Bridgecroft Beer Supplies were handed the task of finding a brewer to make a special bottled beer for the event. The committee's requirements were not on a large enough scale to interest the major brewers but the Hambleton Brewery in Thirsk, North Yorkshire, came up with a traditional Yorkshire bitter that could be bottled and sold as *Denby D'Ale*. Collectors have kept many of these bottles, though it must be said that very few remain full. A souvenir brochure was also sold on pie day for £2.

Some of the earlier items of memorabilia have now gained not inconsequential value. Plates from 1887 and 1896 are relatively rare, though their worth largely depends upon their condition. Old photographs can sell for anything up to £20 each, but again, the value depends on their rarity. Items from the later pies have yet to become valuable but as time moves on and natural wastage reduces their numbers their value will begin to increase. Hang on to any items in your collection and they may well become heirlooms for your grandchildren. Please note that this chapter is not meant to be a complete record of all the items of memorabilia produced over the years but is intended as a guide to the variety of items manufactured.

The large display cabinet at the Pie Hall houses many rare items of memorabilia and more is kept in the members' bar area.

Appendices

Appendix 1

The individuals chosen to ceremonially cut open the pies

1788	Unknown
1815	George Wilby (1797-1872) (suggested possibility)
1846	James Peace (1806-1885)
1887 (1)	Henry Josiah Brierley (1863-1909) in whose absence his father John Brierley (1832-1893) actually cut the pie
1887 (2)	George William Naylor (1845-1888) gave the speech and a team of four carvers took the responsibility: J H Dewsnap, W Holmes, D Mathews and W Lister
1896	Frank Naylor (1874-1943)
1928	William Wood (1859-1934)
1964	Jonas Kenyon (1890-1978)
1988	John Norman Hinchliffe (1928-1995)
2000	Harold Dennis (Dickie) Bird MBE (1933 – present)

Appendix 2

Period of years between each pie

From	To	Time Period (years)
1788	1815	27
1815	1846	31
1846	1887	41
1887	1896	9
1896	1928	32
1928	1964	36
1964	1988	24
1988	2000	12

Appendix 3

Ingredients of each pie:

1788	unknown
1815	20 fowls, 2 sheep and half a peck of flour.
1846	44½ stones of flour, 19lbs lard, 16lbs butter, 7 hares, 14 rabbits, 4 pheasants, 4 grouse, 2 ducks, 2 geese, 2 turkeys, 2 guinea fowls, 4 hens, 6 pigeons, 63 small birds, 5 sheep, 1 calf, 100lbs beef.
1887 (1)	1,581lbs beef, 163lbs veal, 180lbs lamb, 180lbs mutton, 250lbs lean pork, 40 pigeons, 42 fowls, 3 hares, 64 rabbits, 12 grouse, 21 ducks, 4 plovers, 1 turkey, 5 geese, 2 wild ducks, 108 small birds, 20lbs suet, 42 stones potatoes.
1887 (2)	48 stones flour, 96 stones potatoes, 1 heifer, 2 calves, 2 sheep.
1896	1,120lbs beef, 180lbs veal, 112lbs mutton, 60lbs lamb, 1,120lbs flour, 160lbs lard.
1928	4 bullocks, 600lbs beef, 15 cwt potatoes, 80 stones flour, 2 cwt lard, 2 stones baking powder.
1964	3 tons beef, 1½ tons potatoes, ½ ton gravy and seasoning, ½ ton flour, ½ ton lard.
1988	3,000kg beef, 3,000kg potatoes, 700kg onions, 700kg gravy & spices, 1,500kg flour, 1,200kg margarine.
2000	4,864kg beef, 3,786kg water, 2,233kg potatoes, 1,008kg onions, 164kg John Smiths bitter, 105kg herbs.

Appendix 4

Location of pie oven and pie field

1788	White Hart Inn, Denby Dale	Cliff Style Field
1815	Corn Mill, Denby Dale	Unknown
1846	Cuckstool Farm, Denby Dale	Norman Park
1887 (1)	White Hart Inn, Denby Dale	Norman Park
1887 (2)	White Hart Inn, Denby Dale	Inkerman Mill
1896	Corn Mill, Denby Dale	Norman Park
1928	Corn Mill, Denby Dale	Norman Park
1964	Dry Hill Farm, Lower Denby	Norman Park
1988	Broomfield House, Upper Denby	Coal Pit Lane Fields, off Barnsley Road
2000	Dry Hill Farm, Lower Denby	Dry Hill Farm

NB1: *Cliff Stile was spelt thus on the Ordnance Survey map of 1854, before this it is likely that the spelling varied slightly – Cliffe Style.*
NB2: *Norman Park had, by 1964, become locally referred to as the Pie Field, after all this was the fifth pie to be eaten there. Norman Park encompassed the fields behind Inkerman Farm (now Inkerman Court) opposite the site formerly Inkerman Mill on the Barnsley Road or Kaye Line*

Appendix 5

Size of the pie dish by year and gross weight

1788	unknown	unknown
1815	unknown	unknown
1846	7 feet 10 inches diameter, 22 inches deep.	unknown
1887	8 feet diameter, 2 feet deep.	approx 1½ tons.
1887	8 feet diameter, 2 feet deep.	approx 2 tons.
1896	8 feet diameter, 2 feet deep.	approx 1.75 tons.
1928	16 feet long, 5 feet wide, 15 inches deep.	approx 4 tons gross.
1964	18 feet long, 6 feet wide, 18 inches deep.	7 tons gross.
1988	20 feet long, 7 feet wide, 1½ feet deep.	9. 03 tonnes.
2000	40 feet long, 9 feet wide, 3 feet deep.	12.10 tonnes.

Appendix 6

The final resting places of the pie dishes

1788	Stand pie – no dish.
1815	Stand pie – no dish.
1846	Stand pie – no dish.
1887 & 1896	Melted down as scrap during World War Two.
1928	Buried in a field behind the viaduct and used as a dew pond.
1964	Mounted outside the Pie Hall and used as an ornamental flowerbed.
1988	Used as a huge planter in a butterfly garden at Gilthwaites First School.
2000	Kept on private land near Denby Dale.

Selected Sources

Barnsley Chronicle.
Denby Dale Pie Souvenir Brochures 1887, 1896, 1964, 1988 and 2000.
Denby & District Volume III – Chris Heath – 2006.
Huddersfield Examiner.
Huddersfield District Chronicle.
Leeds Mercury.
The History of the Denby Dale Pies – Chris Heath – 1998.
The Denby Dale Pies – An Illustrated Narrative History – David Bostwick – 1988.
The Mammoth Pies of Denby Dale – Norah Kitson – 1964.
Yorkshire Observer.

Epilogue

SANDON

Lead, kindly Light, amid th'encircling gloom, lead Thou me on!
The night is dark, and I am far from home; lead Thou me on!
Keep Thou my feet; I do not ask to see
The distant scene; one step enough for me.
I was not ever thus, nor prayed that Thou shouldst lead me on;
I loved to choose and see my path; but now lead Thou me on!
I loved the garish day, and, spite of fears,
Pride ruled my will. Remember not past years!
So long Thy power hath blest me, sure it still will lead me on.
O'er moor and fen, o'er crag and torrent, till the night is gone,
And with the morn those angel faces smile, which I
Have loved long since, and lost awhile!
Meantime, along the narrow rugged path, Thyself hast trod,
Lead, Saviour, lead me home in childlike faith, home to my God.
To rest forever after earthly strife
In the calm light of everlasting life.

In remembrance of the four 'pie' men
who died on 31 August 1964

Benjamin Beever
John Schofield Haigh
George Saville
Laurence Wainwright